ANF ENFIELD LIBRARIES

The Origins of Wizards, Witches and Fairies

The Origins of Wizards, Witches and Fairies

Simon Webb

AN IMPRINT OF PEN & SWORD BOOKS LTD
YORKSHIRE - PHILADELPHIA

First published in Great Britain in 2022 by
Pen & Sword History
An imprint of
Pen & Sword Books Ltd
Yorkshire - Philadelphia

Copyright © Simon Webb, 2022

ISBN 978 1 39900 007 9

The right of Simon Webb to be identified as the Author of this work has been asserted by him in accordance with the Copyright, Designs and Patents Act 1988.

A CIP catalogue record for this book is available from the British Library.

All rights reserved. No part of this book may be reproduced or transmitted in any form or by any means, electronic or mechanical including photocopying, recording or by any information storage and retrieval system, without permission from the Publisher in writing.

Printed and bound in England
by CPI Group (UK) Ltd, Croydon, CR0 4YY

Pen & Sword Books Ltd incorporates the Imprints of Pen & Sword Archaeology, Atlas, Aviation, Battleground, Discovery, Family History, History, Maritime, Military, Naval, Politics, Railways, Select, Transport, True Crime, Fiction, Frontline Books, Leo Cooper, Praetorian Press, Seaforth Publishing, Wharncliffe and White Owl.

For a complete list of Pen & Sword titles please contact

PEN & SWORD BOOKS LIMITED
47 Church Street, Barnsley, South Yorkshire, S70 2AS, England
E-mail: enquiries@pen-and-sword.co.uk
Website: www.pen-and-sword.co.uk

London Borough of Enfield	
91200000765023	
Askews & Holts	04-May-2022
133.4309	
ENWINC	

Contents

List of Illustrations   vi

Introduction   viii

Chapter 1   The Magical Realm   1

Chapter 2   Tales from the Magical Realm   10

Chapter 3   Echoes of the Past   25

Chapter 4   The Coming of the Yamnaya   40

Chapter 5   In Search of The Horned God   55

Chapter 6   The First Wizard   68

Chapter 7   The Wild Hunt   80

Chapter 8   The Place of Wizards in Society   87

Chapter 9   Of Cauldrons and Wands   102

Chapter 10   On the Nature of Fairies   114

Chapter 11   How Christianity made Wizardry Disreputable   132

Chapter 12   Ritual Sacrifice in Modern Britain   147

Chapter 13   Our Cultural Heritage   164

Appendix: The Magical Year   175

Bibliography   **187**

Index   **189**

List of Illustrations

1. A modern version of the wizard's hat, with which we are all familiar.
2. A golden hat, dating back 3,000 years, bearing astronomical symbols.
3. The so-called 'Witch of Subeshi', wearing a hat which was made over 2,000 years ago. (Jeffrey Newbury)
4. Witches as shown in an old woodcut, wearing the immediately recognizable black, pointed hats.
5. The sword Excalibur is hurled into the lake.
6. Horned helmet recovered from the River Thames in London. (Ealdgyth)
7. Rumpelstiltskin, delighted at the prospect of acquiring a human baby.
8. Medieval stone coffin in London's Southwark Cathedral, with tribute of coins.
9. The 'Sorcerer of Trois-Frères', a prehistoric shaman.
10. The Lord of the Animals as depicted on the Gundestrup Cauldron.
11. Cernunnos, the Horned God, as shown on a 2,000-year-old carving. (ChrisO)
12. A seventeenth-century Siberian shaman enacts rituals to aid in the hunting of horned animals.
13. Deer skull used as a head-dress in Britain, 10,000 years ago. (BBC)
14. The Dagenham Idol. (Ethan Doyle White)
15. The god Pan, a later avatar of Cernunnos.

16. One of the so-called 'bog bodies', sacrificial victims from the Iron Age.
17. An ancient god rides upon his cult animal.
18. The Horned God visits a nineteenth-century home to punish sinful children.
19. A human acquires antlers and changes from hunter to quarry.
20. Statue of Queen Victoria and Prince Albert tricked out like medieval monarchs.

Introduction

Wizards and witches have been a much-loved staple of English literature for as far back as one cares to look. From Merlin in the old tales of King Arthur's court to the Harry Potter books and all the way through to the *Game of Thrones* television series, everybody loves wizards. The curious thing is that we all have a very clear idea in our minds of just what wizards and witches ought to look like, just as we also instinctively know something about fairies, goblins and dwarves. We understand too something of the dispositions and natures of these non-existent beings. Witches are a pretty malevolent bunch on the whole. Wizards are usually good, although there are some rogues among them. Fairies are nice, but goblins are mischievous and mean. Dwarves are greedy and grasping. This is, when you think about, very odd. We all have an extensive knowledge about all kinds of people and strange entities whom we have never actually encountered in real life. One or two examples will make this a little clearer.

Both the book of *The Lord of the Rings* and the three films based upon it were tremendously popular. The narrative contains many heroic characters, ranging from Aragorn to Frodo Baggins, but one person in particular stands out and has always been a favourite with readers and moviegoers. This is of course the wizard Gandalf. Something about the wandering man of magic with his long white beard, pointed hat and staff seemed to strike a chord with almost everybody. Gandalf is the very archetype of a wizard and he is instantly recognizable as such. This is how he was introduced to the world in *The Hobbit*, a children's book which Tolkien wrote before *The Lord of the Rings*;

> All that the unsuspecting Bilbo saw that morning was an old man with a staff. He had a tall pointed blue hat, a long grey cloak, a silver scarf over which his long white beard hung down below his waist, and immense black boots.

How do we know immediately, before reading any further, that a mysterious old man with a white beard, carrying a walking staff, wearing a grey cloak and with a pointed hat on his head is likely to be a wizard? It is because almost anybody born and brought up in Europe has, at the back of his or her mind, various archetypes or templates for certain figures, one of whom is the wandering magician. It is at these strange images, which we all carry as part of our cultural baggage, that we shall be looking in this book.

Before going any further, it should be made plain that these ideas about the appearance and conduct of wizards and elves are not limited to the British Isles, although for geographical reasons they have been preserved with the greatest fidelity in what is sometimes known as the 'Celtic Fringe', that is to say Cornwall, Wales, Western Scotland and Ireland. They are relics of very old European traditions, which by a happy accident of topography have lingered on in the furthermost edge of Europe until the present day. Indeed, in that European country which is furthest from the mainland, these beliefs have survived almost unaffected by the modern world. A survey in 1998 revealed that over half the population of that country, 54.4 per cent, still believed in elves. Nor is this a vague, whimsical or theoretical belief. When plans were announced for the building of a road through the Alftanes peninsula, near the Icelandic capital of Reykjavik, there were widespread protests. The reason was that local residents thought that elves living in the area would be disturbed and have their lives disrupted by the construction work.

Here is a question similar to that which we asked about the appearance of wizards. If, when we see children going out to trick-or-treat at Halloween, we should happen to spot a little girl dressed from head to toe in black and with a pointy black hat on her head, we know at once that she is supposed to be a witch. How? This is another stereotypical idea about the appearance of wizards and witches, but where did it come from? At first sight, this may seem like a trivial and easily-answered question. We have all of us seen pictures of wizards and witches in books, and also watched them being represented in plays, films and computer games. The pointed hats, grey cloaks for men and black clothes for witches are just part of our cultural backdrop, aren't they? This of course only takes the problem back a generation or two. When a film like *The Wizard of Oz* was made 80 years ago, the idea of what constituted the appearance of a witch was already fixed in the public mind. The people who dressed up actresses as witches for that film must already have had a clear idea in their own minds of what a witch should look like. They in turn gained their images from an earlier source, presumably the same one upon which Tolkien drew in order to describe the wizard Gandalf. Just how far back does this process go? In other words, where and when did these visual representations originate? The answer is surprising, even a little terrifying.

Illustration 1 shows part of a fancy-dress costume. It is a wizard's hat decorated with images of stars. Some novelties of this kind have other celestial bodies on them, the sun and moon for instance. This is very much the sort of thing which we might expect to see perched on the head of a wizard; it fits in perfectly with the archetypes we have been discussing. If we turn now to Illustration 2, we can see another wizard's hat. It is immediately familiar to us and is just the kind of hat that Gandalf wore in *The Lord of the Rings*. It too is decorated with what are assumed to be astronomical symbols, representations of the sun or moon. The shocking thing about this piece of headgear is its age, for it was made over 3,000 years ago, almost certainly for a shaman or wizard. Illustration 3 shows the body of a woman wearing another pointed hat. This is black; it is just like a witch's hat that you might see today at Halloween. The owner of this hat died over 2,000 years ago.

Illustration 4 is an old woodcut from the seventeenth century which shows witches with their traditional headgear, dancing with demons.

In this book we shall be looking at where our ideas about wizards, witches and fairies came from. To do this, we will have to look at archaeological discoveries, examine new research in genetics and, perhaps most importantly of all, study the folklore and legends which have accumulated in Europe since the Bronze Age, many of which have been successfully transplanted to another continent and now flourish in the United States and Canada. One thinks, for example of Washington Irving's story of *Rip Van Winkle*, in which a man is mysteriously transported to a place where time travels at a different rate and returns to his own world after the passage of 20 years. This is an exceedingly ancient Celtic legend about fairies, reworked into an American setting.

We will also be exploring a strange, but at the same time eerily familiar, landscape; one in which we all feel quite at home, despite never having visited. This is the world, the stage if you like, upon which wizards and witches, along with fairies, dragons and heroic warriors, act out their lives. We know this place not only from the fairy tales which were read to us as children, but also from books like *The Lord of the Rings*, *The Lion, the Witch and the Wardrobe* and more recently *Game of Thrones.* The fascination which the television series made from the *Game of Thrones* books held for millions of people is testament to the enduring fascination which this land holds for us.

It is this setting, which might be described as the magical realm, which will be the subject of the first chapter. At risk of giving a spoiler, it is a central contention of this book that such a place once existed in reality, although on a much more modest scale and without any of the supernatural elements which have crept in over the millennia. It is the folk memory which provides us with one of our most potent geographical archetypes; the world of heroes, wizards and fairies. It is time to enter and explore the magical realm.

Chapter 1

The Magical Realm

We live in the most technologically advanced society ever known, full of wonders which would have been unimaginable only a generation ago. Every bit of our world has been mapped, catalogued and photographed. From our mobile telephones or laptops, it is possible to summon up satellite pictures of any part of the earth's surface and to zoom in and see what every city, forest, desert and plain looks like. With the GPS facility on our phones, being lost or out of touch with other people is unheard of for most of us in our day-to-day lives. There are of course great advantages to this lifestyle, but there is also a downside, a price to be paid. This lies in the loss of wonder; the realization that the world is no longer a mysterious place and that no hiding place is left for anything much out of the ordinary, whether it is the Loch Ness Monster or the lost valley of Shangri-La in the Himalayas. If these things existed, then we would spot them on Google Earth or on some webcam or other. This goes some way toward explaining the attraction of an alternative world, which is still largely unmapped and where one might stumble across the most amazing people and places, even go where no man or woman has ever set foot before. Unknown creatures dwell there, as well as races other than humans.

The strange thing is not that so many of us have a vague desire for such alluring and magical lands, which we encounter in books, films and computer games and seem to be so much more attractive than our own, it is that the features of these imaginary worlds almost invariably conform to the same parameters. In other words, we do not all dream up completely individual fantasies of this kind, but tend instead to use a broadly similar template or pattern. When we read fantasy fiction, watch a television series or film, or play a computer game, we subconsciously judge them against a common framework. The film version of *The Lord of the Rings* was so successful for this very reason; that it resembled closely the magical world with which most of us are already subconsciously familiar. The television series *Game of Thrones* was set in a similar universe of wizards, dragons and warriors. Fiction of this kind strikes a chord in those of European heritage and it sometimes seems that we are unthinkingly comparing narratives like these with some original of which we are only vaguely aware. A more recent example of this appeal of the lost world may be found in the Disney film *Maleficent*. The features of this landscape may be traced from the Arthurian legends, through to *Grimm's Fairy Tales* and then on to the world of *The Lion, the Witch and the Wardrobe*. Let us pause for a moment and consider what this imaginary country, for which we feel a wistful longing, is like.

The first thing which we observe is that this is a pre-industrial era. Technology has not advanced beyond the spinning wheel and blacksmith's forge. Machinery is wholly unknown. At the very latest, we might be looking at the medieval period, but it is altogether possible it is centuries, or even millennia, earlier than this. The land is largely untamed, with vast primeval forests and moors haunted by bears, wolves and other, even stranger creatures such as dragons or men who can change at will into ferocious beasts. There are few, if any, cities. Most people live in villages surrounded by cultivated fields. Here and there are strongholds and castles of local chieftains and warlords, some of whom style themselves princes or even kings. These leaders range from wise and kind to capricious and cruel.

The laws of nature in this universe are precisely the same as in our own. Those living there must eat and therefore grow crops and keep sheep and cattle, as well as hunting wild animals such as boar. The climate is temperate, with the same seasons with which we are familiar. The further north one travels, the colder it gets. There are no deserts or jungles and in general what we see of the flora and fauna put us in mind of Europe rather than any other of the continents which we know. The force of gravity is roughly the same as that found on Earth, night alternates with day and men and women have a natural lifespan. They grow old and die or can be killed in wars. This is not some land of wish-fulfilment, where everybody is happy or immortal. Some people are rich and others poor. There are beggars and princes. In between these two extremes are the mass of ordinary people, the warriors, farmers, craftsmen and their families. In addition to these human inhabitants whose abilities are much the same as our own, there are various other individuals who are possessed of strange powers. These are the wizards and witches. Wizards are usually solitary beings, often wanderers with no permanent home. They very commonly carry staffs, wands or sceptres, long stick-like objects endowed with special power. Witches are sometimes a little more gregarious. One would not expect to find three or four wizards working together, but half a dozen witches might very well cooperate to cast some especially powerful spell. They may use cauldrons when conjuring up a particularly potent enchantment.

The society which lives in this strange world is divided into three different classes or castes, an important point to which we shall later return in greater detail. These are wizards or priests – the two categories are sometimes interchangeable – warriors, and ordinary farmers and workers. Although on rare occasions a member of the labouring classes might aspire to, or even achieve, the ambition of becoming a warrior or wizard, the reverse never happens. The idea of a knight or wandering man of magic working for a living like anybody else is unthinkable.

This is not of course, as has already been remarked, some place of wish-fulfilment – still less is it any sort of paradise. There is misery, sickness and poverty and the lengths of the lives of men and women are strictly limited. Nor is it the Land of Eternal Youth or any other form of mystical afterworld. People grow old and die, misfortunes befall them, they are hungry and thirsty, life can be hard, with no promise of reward. If you wanted to dream up a fantasy world where everybody is happy and content and all our troubles melt away, this is not what you would come up with. Life here is as arduous, disappointing and hazardous as it is in the real world. It is important to realize this; if you were setting out to invent a heaven where we would all live happily ever after, this would not be the sort of scenario you would devise.

It was remarked above that the physical world imposes the same constraints upon those living in what might be termed the magical realm as in this world; but under certain circumstances these may be evaded or overthrown. In our world, of course, we can defy gravity or prolong life by means of machinery based on scientific principles – spaceships, jet aircraft and heart transplants to give a few examples. In this other world, the laws of nature can be bent by the use of magic. If anybody wishes to travel through the air, it might be done not by going to an airport but rather by means of dragons, flying carpets or broomsticks.

The humans often seem to share their world with other races, each of which has distinctive characteristics. In mines and caves live the small, dark dwarves, who are often surly and overly fond of gold. Then there are the fays or fairies, beings who live in the woodland and are seldom glimpsed by the humans.

We have described above what might loosely be thought of as fairy tale land. It is the setting for most traditional stories like *Beauty and the Beast*, *Snow White* and all the rest that we remember from childhood. It is also where the Hobbits live and one would not be at all surprised to bump into Gandalf there, or Merlin, King Arthur or, for that matter, the cast of *Game of Thrones*! All of them would be quite at home in the land we have just looked at. Which, when you think about it, is more than a little odd. To those listed above who would not be out of place, we can add all the characters from C.S. Lewis's Narnia books, many of those from Terry Pratchett's Discworld novels, the cast of Wagner's Ring Cycle, the men from *Beowulf* and the men and women from Middle English classics like *Sir Gawain and the Green Knight* or Thomas Mallory's *Le Morte d'Arthur*.

So powerful is the attraction of this imaginary landscape and so universal the themes and characters found within it – the heroic warrior on a quest, the solitary wizard, the Little People and so on – that it appears likely that the whole thing, stage and actors both, has a common origin. This cannot lie in the literature of the past, for already the earliest written versions of this world are clearly based upon one original. The Icelandic *Eddas*, *Le Morte d'Arthur*, the fairy tale of *Beauty and the Beast* – none of these can be the source of the original images. All draw though from that source, which undoubtedly lies in the pre-literate past.

Having sketched out the topography and described some of the inhabitants of the world of fantasy and fairy tales as we know it today, I want to talk a little about a broadly similar landscape which actually did exist and see if there might be a connection between the two. Having done so, we can make a comparison between these places and see if one might have been the inspiration for the other.

Picture, if you will, a space roughly the size of a continent, corresponding, as a matter of interest, to the dimensions of Middle Earth in the maps drawn by Tolkien's son Christopher for the first edition of *The Lord of the Rings*. In the north of this huge territory are frozen wastes and, just as in our own world, the further south one travels, the warmer it becomes. For this reason, those living here regard the right hand as wholesome and good and the left-hand path as bad and undesirable. This is because they orient themselves not by facing north, as we do, but east. The right-hand way then leads to warmer and more pleasant climes and the left to the inhospitable wastelands in the north. Working out directions by reference to the north is connected with our use of magnetic compasses, a technology which was not to be found in the place at which we are looking.

There are no cities in the largely unexplored and wild forests, plains and mountains, merely small villages and a scattering of farmsteads. In that respect, it might perhaps be compared to the American West of the mid-nineteenth century. The parallel is a pleasing and appropriate one, for most of those living here are not the indigenous inhabitants. They came originally from the east, which is why they face towards their homeland when they orient themselves for direction. Here and there are forts or castles, some of which are ruled over by men who view themselves as kings.

In modern society, there are strict delineations between the real world and the spiritual, between the living and the dead, between fact and fiction. No such distinction exists here. Some rivers and lakes are inhabited by local deities who must be placated, in case they snatch children and drag them under the water to drown. The dead can be a menace as well, because they do not automatically leave the world of the living after their hearts stop beating. Some of them linger on or return and cause misfortune to those still living. They too must be treated with respect and propitiated. Gods sometimes adopt human form and walk the earth. Offending such a one can bring ruin upon a family.

Luckily, there are men and women who can help people to keep on the right side of the angry and vengeful dead and know too how to keep both the elder gods and the minor deities happy, so that they will look favourably upon the farms and cause the crops to grow in due season. The men who undertake these religious and magical duties are wizards and they can be distinguished by the tall, pointed hats which they wear, as well as by the wands or staffs which they carry with them. They interpret the will of the gods and sometimes predict the future by various methods of divination. They also explain which sacrifices must be made to ensure that the earth continues to yield a good harvest and that enemies are kept at bay.

One example of the sort of sacrifice which is regularly advised has a familiar ring to it. In the story of King Arthur, as it has come down to us, he is the possessor of an important sword called Excalibur. As he lies wounded and at the point of death, he orders his companion to take Excalibur and hurl it into a nearby lake. When this is done, a woman's arm rises up from the water and catches the hilt of the sword, before brandishing it three times and then sinking back into the lake with it. It has been caught by the mysterious 'Lady of the Lake', either an enchantress or perhaps a primeval deity of the water. This scene may be seen in Illustration 5.

This story of the Lady of the Lake and the sword thrown into the water for her is a well-known one, but strikes us today as bizarre in the extreme. Why ever would anybody throw a perfectly good sword, especially a famous one like this, into a lake? It makes no sense in the real world. But for those living in the world at which we are now looking, it made perfect sense to be ready and willing to give up a precious object in this way, if it meant keeping gods, wizards and witches on your side. They often sacrificed weaponry in this way, by depositing it in rivers and lakes. Their swords, shields and helmets were very important to them, luxury items which would today be the equivalent of a new sports car, but if it meant showing gratitude for victory in a battle or a plentiful harvest, then they did not hesitate. Some pools near their villages were clogged up with dozens of swords. In Illustration 6 we see a bronze helmet which was sacrificed in just this way by being deposited in the River Thames in London.

Rites like this, when people would gather to give up something which was very precious and important to them, were key to understanding this society. It was a hazardous and uncertain land, where dangers lurked at every turn. Those perils came in many forms and it was not always easy to recognize the true nature of either animals or men or women. A shabby-looking individual with his face concealed by a hood might be a wandering tramp, but he might equally well turn out to be a wizard or even a god.

Outside the villages and on the edge of civilized and tamed farmland live wolves, bears and large cats. Even these are not always what they seem. Some of these ferocious beasts are really men who have used magic to transform themselves into animals. Such men might farm their fields by day and then turn into wolves at night, especially during a full moon. One can never be sure of strangers. An old beggar-woman may turn out to be a beautiful enchantress in disguise, while an old man walking the roads might be the king of the gods, visiting the earth to see how his subjects are behaving. For this reason, it is wise to be hospitable to lone travellers and to give alms to beggars. Those who neglect these duties have sometimes been cursed by a witch or punished by the gods.

At night, when the work was done, the villagers would listen to stories and the re-telling of legends. Sometimes they would tell each other tales of long ago, but the wizards who visited them were also professional bards and they would relate poems and stories to entertain their hosts. Some of these are still known to us today. *Beauty and the Beast* was one of them and the idea of a fairy causing a man to be changed into a hideous animal caused no raised eyebrows, for all those listening had heard of similar cases. *Rumpelstiltskin* was also a favourite, because there too one of the Little People played a central role.

Stories about the 'good folk' or 'hidden people' struck a chord with those in this world, because they were as much a real and present danger as the wolves which sometimes carried away lambs from their flocks. Sometimes babies would be stolen away by the fairies or they might raid an orchard and take all the apples from the trees. Tools and farm implements could be stolen at night. Younger people believed the Little People to be supernatural beings, but some of the older villagers remembered that they themselves were relative newcomers to the land and that they had driven out the original inhabitants, killing most of them. A remnant lingered on though, eking out a wretched existence in forests and caves, conducting low-key guerrilla operations against the invaders by kidnapping their children and engaging in acts of minor terrorism.

The two worlds at which we have looked in this chapter are so similar as to be all but indistinguishable. It takes no great leap of faith to believe that one is derived from the other. The second of the two descriptions given above is of Bronze Age Europe and although a little imagination and colour has been added and a few shrewd guesses made to fill in one or two blanks, the facts are presented pretty much as the most recent work in archaeology and genetics suggest.

Of course, the question we must next address is the extent to which it is reasonable to believe that we most of us have in our minds an image of European life in the Bronze Age, some 4,000 years ago, and that this exerts a powerful influence upon our choice of television programme or the computer games which we play. This sounds, on the face of it, a little fanciful. A later chapter will deal with the way in which memories may be passed down by word of mouth for hundreds, possibly thousands, of years. The story of Excalibur and the Lady of the Lake is a good instance of this. The practice of Bronze Age weapons being consigned to rivers and lakes ended at or before the Roman occupation of Britain. The first written account of Arthur's sword being deposited in a lake in the same way may be found over 1,000 years later. Assuming that it is not mere coincidence, which seems unlikely for such a peculiar incident, and that it was indeed based upon the sacrifice of swords and other war-gear to spirits and fairies of the water, then stories of this practice must have been passed down from generation to generation and kept alive purely by word of mouth. We begin by examining the influence of the short stories which were dreamed up in an attempt to make sense of the world in which they lived. We know these narratives today as fairy tales, although not all of them by any means feature fairies or elves.

Chapter 2

Tales from the Magical Realm

Talk of 'fairy tales' today and most people will understand us to be referring either to old stories for children or alternatively just lies, 'fairy tales' having become a euphemism for falsehoods. Actually of course, real fairy tales are neither of these things but rather short stories and anecdotes about life and death in what we have described above as the magical realm. 'Fairy tales' is something of a misnomer of course, because not all these tales are about fairies. Rather, they all take place in that strange landscape at which we have been looking. As the author of *The Lord of the Rings* wrote in an essay on the subject called 'On Fairy-Stories', these are 'stories about the adventures of men in Faërie'. In other words, the primary feature of fairy tales is not the Little People or the talking animals which might be found there, but rather the way in which humans interact with these other sentient beings.

It might be worth going off at a slight tangent for a moment to remark that we are so used to the idea of fiction as being a 'thing', that we sometimes forget what a strange idea it is to write whole books about events which never happened. One quite understands why stories about gods and goddesses and foundation myths of nations might be devised and repeated, even though there may not be any more truth in them than there is in the works of fantasy novelists such as Terry Pratchett. Such works serve a useful purpose, perhaps unifying a people and endowing them with an identity. For the Romans, the story of Romulus and Remus being suckled by a she-wolf and of the intrigues and adventures of their pantheon of deities were an integral part of their culture. These legends are not fiction though, at least not in the same way that *Little Red Riding Hood* and *Jane Eyre* are.

Thinking of *Jane Eyre* reminds us that the whole European literary tradition, the idea of novels to give one example, is inextricably linked to what we now dismiss patronizingly as 'fairy tales'. The reason for this is that the themes and plots of those first stories told in Europe are incredibly ancient and are the foundation for the entire storytelling tradition which we now call 'fiction'. The most successful and beloved of classic novels are often merely extended versions of familiar fairy tales. Just how old are those fairy tales which we still relate to our children at bedtime?

In 2016 an article was published in the *Royal Society Open Science* magazine about the origins of some of the most popular and well-known European fairy tales; things such as the story of Rumpelstiltskin and his attempts to get hold of a human baby. Another old story which was studied was *Beauty and the Beast*, a perennial favourite which has been made into two successful films in recent years. Researchers studied themes and language in much the way that the DNA of populations is examined in order to trace the origin of this or that ethnic group. Most of the traditional fairy stories which we know were only written down for the first time as late as the sixteenth century. This has led to the idea that far from being ancient oral traditions, tales like *Beauty and the Beast* are no more than literary creations from the Tudor period.

The methods used to establish the age of stories like *Rumpelstiltskin* are difficult to explain. Essentially, the aim was to distinguish between 'horizontal' and 'vertical' transmission of the basic structures of narratives. Horizontal spread means the way that a particular tale can be spread geographically from one part of the world to another, while vertical transmission refers to the way that it is handed on in the same place by word of mouth. The question studied was whether there was enough evidence to say if the fairy tales had been invented by somebody a few centuries ago and written down or if they might have been handed down in an oral tradition for a lot longer. In the same way that biological inheritance can be studied and measured, so too can language structures.

We shall in this book be looking at the derivation of the languages of Europe, all but three or four of which descend from a single, original language which was being spoken in what is now Ukraine some thousands of years ago. Just as the descent of European and Indian languages may be charted from the original Proto-Indo-European, so too were differing versions of the fairy tales in languages as varied as Greek, Russian, Hindi and Welsh by those conducting the study, the results of which were published in 2016. The variations were contrasted and compared and a family tree put together, showing how the narrative structure had altered over time and across space. The conclusions reached by this meticulous study were absolutely breath-taking. The story of *Jack and the Beanstalk* was found to be part of a family of tales which could be summarized as 'The Boy who Stole the Ogre's Treasure'. The original of this family of stories, versions of which can be found as far afield as Iran and India, was circulating about 5,000 years ago, just at the time that the Proto-Indo-European language was splitting into western and eastern branches. In other words, a staple of bedtime stories and British pantomimes was being told around hearths during the Bronze Age. *Beauty and the Beast* proved to be a little more recent, dating only from around 2000 BC. One story though, *The Smith and the Devil*, turned out to be the oldest of all.

Versions of *The Smith and the Devil* are to be found across the whole of Europe and much of south Asia, as far east as Bangladesh. A worker in metal, iron in later stories although possibly copper or bronze in the earliest iterations of the tale, makes a deal with a malevolent supernatural being. After the coming of Christianity to Europe, the being is identified as the Devil, but in other cultures he can be a genie or other evil spirit. The deal entails the smith or metalworker gaining great power in exchange for his soul. The idea of somebody making a pact with the Devil in this way is of course a fairly common one in folklore. There is even an adjective for such transactions; Faustian. This is from the story of Faust, who made such an agreement with the Devil which he ended up regretting. *The Smith and the Devil* has rather a different ending, because the human manages to outwit the entity with whom he entered into the arrangement. One of the powers which the smith received in exchange for his soul was the ability to weld or braze an object to any other thing he chose. For a man working at a forge, this would of course be a very useful skill to possess. The first use which the smith made of his new ability was to fix the Devil to a tree, so that he would never be able to come and collect the smith's soul.

All the indications are that this story was passed down by word of mouth from an original which was first told 6,000 years ago. Returning now to *Beauty and the Beast*, a relative youngster which is probably no more than 4,000 years old, we consider what was said above about stories of this kind being the inspiration for, and foundation of, most of the literature which we have subsequently seen in Europe. Some readers may have thought this claim a little fanciful, but consider for a moment the essential feature of *Beauty and the Beast*. It boils down to this, an innocent young woman, a virgin, comes to a large house or castle which is inhabited by a man under some tragedy or enchantment which makes him behave like a beast at times. She falls in love with him and the enchantment or sadness is lifted and he becomes an ordinary, loving husband.

We have here the theme of *Jane Eyre*, of course. The same thing happens, with the virgin going to live in the huge house in a remote location. The place is ruled by a man under some kind of spell, which causes him to be sometimes unpleasant and at other times sad. He is redeemed by the maiden's love and they live happily ever after. This plot also forms the basis for the film *The Sound of Music*, of course. Another example would be Daphne du Maurier's *Rebecca*. There is something about the idea of the virgin and the intimidating man under a curse or enchantment which appeals to us, even in the twenty-first century.

Just as we tend to judge fantasy novels and films according how closely they align with a subconscious mental pattern to which we compare them, so too do we use a similar process when evaluating all fiction, by seeking familiar points of reference. It may be a startling revelation that the enduring success of a film like *The Sound of Music* owes a debt to a fable dating back to the Bronze Age, but the same can be said of many other novels, films and television series. The child with mysterious parentage is such an idea and has contributed in no small measure to the enormous popularity of the books about Harry Potter, to give one example.

Merlin is a key player in one of the earliest versions which we have of the child who has unknown parents and turns out to be more important than anybody could guess. Those familiar with the legends associated with King Arthur will know that his father was King Uther. Because the times were so perilous and Uther feared that harm might befall his baby son, he entrusted the child to Merlin, who promised to make sure that he would grow up safely. Merlin placed the child with a foster family, Sir Ector and his son Kay. Arthur grew up not knowing his parents or realizing that he had a special destiny. This theme is one which features often in Indo-European myths; the hero who does not know that he is special. We see it with Achilles and Theseus in Greek mythology, Romulus and Remus in Roman myths and of course, more recently Luke Skywalker in the Star Wars cycle, Aquaman in a recent film of that name and Harry Potter. Wizards and wise men always have a role to play in these stories.

We have seen that some of our fairy tales have their origins 5,000 or 6,000 years ago in the early days of the Bronze Age. It has even been suggested that one old story, that of the swan maiden, might date from the Palaeolithic, that is to say the Old Stone Age which ended over 11,000 years ago. It seems certain that humans have been making up stories about weird events such as a witch imprisoning a young girl in a tower or a little girl wandering into a house occupied by a family of talking bears from before the dawn of civilization. These stories were being told at a time when there was no writing and the people telling them were often living in tents or other makeshift dwelling-places.

The academic study in 2016 to which we referred above examined closely only a few well-known stories. Reading through anthologies of fairy tales which were gathered together in the nineteenth century gives us hints that many more of these stories might contain fragments which date back even before the Bronze Age. One of the stories collected by the Brothers Grimm was called *Der Singende Knochen* or *The Singing Bone*. It relates a story of family rivalry in which two brothers murder a third and bury his corpse under a bridge. Many years pass and the two brothers live prosperous lives. One day a shepherd crossing the bridge notices a white bone laying on the bank of the stream and goes down to pick it up. He fashions the bone into part of a musical instrument, a horn, but when he blows it, the bone sings the story of the dead brother. The shepherd goes to the king and plays his horn to him and once again the bone tells the story of the murdered brother. The tale ends with the king ordering the two surviving brothers to be drowned.

We shall be looking a lot at what have become known as 'bog bodies', that is to say corpses which have been deposited in bogs and marshes, but it is enough to say for now that drowning was a method of execution used in Iron Age Europe, but very rarely since then. The fact that this little story tells about two men being put to death by drowning is intriguing. Even more curious is the idea of a bone being used in this way as a horn or flute. This is definitely not something which we have seen in Europe in historical times and we have to go back a very long way indeed to see anything comparable. In the last 10 or 20 years, a number of flutes have been found by archaeologists in Germany, some dating back 40,000 years to the time when modern humans first arrived in Europe. These are made of bird bones and look very much like a traditional penny whistle. The use of bones for flutes, whistles or horns has not been customary since those days of the Stone Age and it is intriguing to see an old story in which a bone is turned into a musical instrument in this way. It is perhaps not inconceivable that some faint memory of the days when such a practice was known has been passed down orally over the years. Another tantalizing glimpse of the possibility of a very long-lived folk memory is to be found in an English fairy tale.

Just as the Brothers Grimm collected fairy tales in Germany and preserved them in print, so too did people in England. We have good reason to suppose that the fairy tales collected by the Grimms date back 5,000 years or more. It is possible that the same thing is true of some of the old English fairy tales. In 1890 a book called simply *English Fairy Tales* was published in London. These were stories which had been collected by a man called Joseph Jacobs. He wished to set down on paper some of the old stories which had been passed down through families. *The Three Little Pigs* was one of the stories which Jacobs collected. He also wrote down a curious story which was told to him by an old woman in the English county of Suffolk.

Cap o' Rushes was the name given to a story which has echoes of, and contains elements from, both *Cinderella* and *King Lear*. A girl, one of three sisters, is asked by her father how much he loves her; she replies that she loves him as fresh meat loves salt. Furious at what he sees as her coldness and lack of affection, he turns her out of the house. So far, so *King Lear*! It is what happens next which sounds at first quite bizarre. Because she has no coat, the girl makes a hooded cloak from rushes, to protect her from the elements. There is a later part of the story in which she attends a ball anonymously, but it is this cloak of rushes which concerns us. The idea of such an item of clothing seemed like a flight of fancy at the time the story was told and nobody could imagine that anybody would really think rushes or grass would make a decent raincoat! It was a typical little bit of fancy from a fairy tale.

In 1991, just over a hundred years after *Cap o' Rushes* first appeared in print, a strange discovery was made in a glacier on the border between Austria and Italy. This was the mummified body of a man, dressed in outlandish fashion. It turned out that he had died over 5,000 years ago and both his body, clothing, weapons and tools were all perfectly preserved. The strangest item of clothing was a long cape which stretched down to his knees. It was woven entirely of dried grass and looked almost identical to the cloak described in *Cap o' Rushes*. It seems that grass and rushes make very effective waterproof coverings, due to the waxy outer layers on the stalks. This principle is of course exploited in the thatching used on some old houses in rural areas. Could the peculiar cloak in the story of *Cap o' Rushes* be a distant echo of such clothing?

Why did people spend time thinking up short narratives about wizards and witches, or a little man, clearly a fairy or goblin, who tried to force a king's wife to give up her baby to him, as in *Rumpelstiltskin*? After all, they had plenty of more important things to be doing in the evening than sitting around a fire relating anecdotes which they had dreamed up. The answer is that fiction like *Cinderella* and the rest was designed to make us think about our relations with others and guide us to an understanding of how the world works. These stories were created by people who found the world which they inhabited an uncanny and perplexing place and so they hoped to try and make sense of it by posing problems and illustrating solutions to those problems. Working in magical elements such as wizards and talking animals made these narratives easily adaptable by other cultures and nationalities, although that was perhaps not the intention of the original authors.

Let us think about the story of Rumpelstiltskin, still a popular tale to read to children at bedtime. Analysis of this fairy tale indicates that it might first have been told in Europe 4,000 years ago during the Bronze Age. To put this in some kind of perspective, that would be at least a thousand years before Homer composed the *Iliad*. The story is probably familiar enough to most readers, but since it includes a number of features upon which we have touched, the outline may be briefly given as follows.

A king stops as he is riding through a village and happens to speak to the miller. Foolishly hoping to make a good impression, the miller boasts that his daughter can spin straw into gold. The king, seeing how beautiful the girl is, and also being very fond of gold, takes the miller's daughter with him to his stronghold. Once there, he shuts her up at night in a room full of straw and tells her that unless she spins it all into gold before dawn, he will have her executed. The girl is in despair, but an odd little man appears and offers to spin the straw into gold if the miller's daughter will give him a gift. She offers her necklace and he works all night spinning the straw and then, before dawn, takes the necklace and vanishes.

The king is of course delighted with all the gold and the following night the process is repeated, only this time with a larger room filled to the ceiling with straw. Once again, the little man appears and this time the girl gives him her ring in payment and he turns all the straw into gold again.

On the third night, the king tells the miller's daughter that if she can spin the straw in an enormous barn into gold by the morning, he means to marry her. As before, she will be executed if she fails to do so. When the little man appears, the girl has nothing to offer him in exchange for his labour. He says that he will do the necessary work if she agrees to give him her firstborn baby once she is married. She does so, thinking that otherwise she will be dead within a few hours.

A year passes and the miller's daughter has now become queen and has a lovely baby boy. One night, the little man appears to demand the child in payment of the debt. The queen weeps and wails and in the end he says that he will return three times on subsequent nights and that if she can guess his name, then he will agree not to take her baby from her.

The next day the queen sent out a messenger to scour the land seeking unusual names. When the little man came that night, she asked him if his name was Ebenezer and he told her that it was not. She went through all the names that had been collected, but none of them were correct. The next day, the messenger went off again and that night the queen tried all the names he brought back. None of them was the right one. The third day, the messenger returned, saying that he only had been able to find one name he had never heard before. He had been riding through a thick forest and there in a clearing was a little man dancing around a fire. He was singing a song, 'Tonight the queen's baby will be mine, my name she'll never guess, for I am Rumpelstiltskin'. This scene is shown in Illustration 7. That night, when the little man came the queen told him his name. He was so furious that he almost exploded, but kept his end of the bargain and left the queen with her baby.

There is a good deal in this short story to think about and it contains some intriguing features. One thing which is immediately apparent is that this story cannot be fixed in any particular time or place. It might be as late as the nineteenth century or it would fit in just as well with the Middle Ages. There is a domesticated horse, wheat is being ground into flour and fleeces spun into wool. All these things would have been found in the Bronze Age too. This is truly a timeless story. It is plain if nothing else that this is a warning against boasting and pride, especially in the presence of one's social superiors. It was the miller's silly showing off which nearly cost his daughter first her life and then her baby. The message is clear, that when we are speaking to powerful people, we should guard our tongues and not get carried away. This same moral is found in many other cultures of course, besides that of the Indo-Europeans. In the Bible, we are told, 'Do not boast in the presence of the king', which advice may be found in Proverbs 25:6.

Another point which is noticeable is the rule of three. The girl is given three rooms of straw to spin into gold and the little man gives her three days in which to guess his name. The importance of the number three is another of those things which has come down to us over the millennia.

This is one of those old tales in which one of the Little People appears and there are echoes here of the idea of the changeling, the fairies kidnapping a human child. We are not told what Rumpelstiltskin's motive is, but the goblin or fairy very much wants to get hold of a human child. Is there any significance in the fact that this will be the son of a king? Does Rumpelstiltskin mean to raise this child to adulthood or could it be that he wants it as a sacrifice of some kind?

We recall that in the story of Rapunzel, there too a baby was acquired by a person with magical abilities for unknown reasons.

There is a final point here and that is the great importance attached to names. It was thought in ancient times that knowing or pronouncing a person's name gave one a certain power over the named person. According to tradition, fairies do not like being named out loud and prefer to be known by euphemisms like 'the hidden people' or the 'good folk'. We still refer to this magical belief when we say, 'Speak of the Devil, he's sure to appear!' Pronouncing the name out loud of some entity allows one to summon it up and perhaps force it to do our bidding.

The desire to get hold of a human child was not limited to fairies; witches too had a liking for children. The witch in *Hansel and Gretel* of course kidnaps the eponymous hero and heroine simply to eat, but in another story with its roots in Indo-European culture, the witch's desire for a baby is not so clear. This is the 'Maiden in the Tower' theme, of which the best-known example to English readers will be *Rapunzel*. We are never told just why the enchantress threatens the husband and wife into handing over their baby daughter to her, nor why she should immure the child in a tall tower which has no staircase leading up it.

Of course, as is so often the case, the adult looking after her is unable to keep the girl from meeting and having sex with a young man when she reaches adolescence, in this case a prince. Rapunzel innocently reveals what she has been up to by telling her guardian that she cannot understand why her clothes seem to be shrinking. She can hardly fit into her dresses any more. When the witch discovers the truth, she casts Rapunzel out into the wilderness. This is curious, because it suggests that the girl's usefulness to the witch was tied up with her virginity and once she was no longer a virgin, she was no further use.

Rapunzel is another of those very old stories which some researchers think has origins thousands of years ago. A myth from Lithuania about the goddess of the sun Saule might be connected with the matter.

Lithuanian is thought to be the modern language most similar to Proto-Indo-European and the myths preserved in that country until modern times are thought by many scholars to be very close to those brought to Europe by the Yamnaya tribes of Indo-European speaking invaders. We shall be exploring the history of the Yamnaya in a later chapter. According to the Lithuanians, the goddess of the sun was Saule and she had a husband called Menuo. This is of course a reversal of the usual myths of Europe, in which the sun is invariably masculine and the moon feminine. At one point, Saule is kidnaped by a powerful king who imprisons her in a high tower with no stairs.

It is of course perfectly possible that the point of *Rapunzel* is no more complicated than to show that however closely you try to protect a young girl and keep her away from boys, nature will find a way to bring them together. There is no doubt that few parents reading the original version of the story, rather than the bowdlerized one usually found in children's books, can resist a wry smile when they reach the part where Rapunzel manages to get pregnant even when locked up in a tower without stairs.

All the older fairy tales take place in the same timeless world, which in itself causes one to suspect their antiquity. We find horses and wagons, but no clocks; spinning wheels, but never gunpowder; kings and queens, but no parliaments; knights, but not police officers. There is nothing at all in any of the traditional stories which would negate an ancient origin, that much at least is certain.

Let us look at two more of the very oldest fairy tales. *Jack and the Beanstalk* tells of the good fortune of a boy who at first sight appears to be a little simple. His mother sends him off to market to sell a cow and he exchanges the beast with a stranger for nothing more than a handful of beans which he is assured are magic. One cannot but sympathize with his mother when instead of returning home with cash, he hands her instead some beans. As a reward, he is sent to bed without any supper and his mother throws the beans out of the window. In the morning, of course, a huge beanstalk is growing outside the boy's window and he climbs up it to find a land where a huge ogre lives. Once again, we find the rule of three, because the boy makes three visits to the ogre's home, stealing first a bag of gold, then a hen which lays golden eggs and finally a golden harp which can sing by itself.

One recurring theme from such stories is the wicked stepmother. We see her at her worst in *Snow White* and *Cinderella*. The message in these two narratives is clear; step-parents do not love their husbands' children by a former wife and wish to be rid of them by any means possible, up to and including engineering their death. To us in the modern Western world, such an idea is monstrous. After all, this is the age of the blended family and stepchildren are no longer just something one encounters in fairy tales, but have in recent decades become a regular feature of our society. We all know families where children do not live with both biological parents and they are surely as happy and secure as any other children? What on earth does the story of *Cinderella* have to teach us?

The expression 'infanticidal coup' is probably one which is unfamiliar to any readers who do not happen to be ethologists. It refers to the practice of male animals and birds taking as a mate a female who already has offspring by another father. From the lions of the Serengeti to the langurs of India, the usual practice under such circumstances remains the same. As soon as the new mate moves in, he kills all the babies by the previous male, thus ensuring that his own seed alone will be passed on to the next generation. The females usually acquiesce in this grisly process. How very different from our own methods, where instead of the unwanted young being disposed of swiftly by biting through their throats, slower and gentler techniques usually accomplish the same purpose. Sometimes, of course, the procedure is every bit as determined and energetic as that which takes place in the lions' den. Step-parents are 150 times more likely to kill a baby than is a genetic parent. Ridding the home of stepchildren though is usually done in a less obvious and more socially acceptable way.

Stepchildren are many times more likely to die from all causes than children living with both their biological parents. Road accidents, fires, drowning, even illness; the mortality rate for stepchildren is far higher in every case. At first sight, this is puzzling. Surely step-parents are not deliberately burning down their homes, just to get rid of an annoying child to whom they are not related? Of course, this is not really what is going on, although such deaths are no less part of an infanticidal coup for all that! Imagine that the house catches fire in the middle of the night. Who do you rescue first; your own child or your partner's kid? Almost everybody will first ensure the safety of their own blood and only when this has been done will an attempt be made to save the life of other people's children. The same applies to crossing the road and being alert to the early signs and symptoms of disease such as meningitis; always, parents pay far more attention to the welfare of their own children. This means in practical terms that if a couple have a biological child together and another child who is unrelated to one of the parents who lives with the family, then this child will not be as well cared for as the one who is related to both parents. The child whom they have both created will have two anxious parents watching over its welfare and keeping an eye out for potential danger; the step-child will have only one. It is hardly surprising therefore that the chances of this child being neglected, injured or killed should be so dramatically higher.

It is clear that if we want to learn something useful about the modern blended family, then reading old fairy tales, older than recorded history, would be a better bet than listening to the soothing pronouncements of twenty-first century sociologists and psychologists! Modern step-parents are every bit as hazardous to the life and well-being of their partner's children as the wicked characters in *Snow White*, *Hansel and Gretel* or *Cinderella*. There is a reason why these old narratives are still so popular.

The fairy tales at which we have been looking provide one important source of the vivid images and nostalgic memories which so many of us feel for the world sketched in Chapter 1. Old wives' tales, fairy stories, books that we loved in our childhoods; all these enable us to construct an image of the magical realm. The written stories which describe the world of wizards and elves, warriors and witches, often derive not from the imagination of some writer, but instead from the memories of actual incidents which have been handed down by word of mouth for thousands of years. These are known as 'folk memories', oral accounts told from mothers and fathers to their children, who then as adults pass on in turn these tales to their own children. Although there is opportunity for such memories to become distorted, or even garbled, the main parts of a narrative are often preserved. In this way, when we read fairy tales or old legends about King Arthur and Merlin, we are sometimes provided with a window into the past. The hurling of the sword Excalibur into a lake is an example of this. We are almost certainly, when reading of this incident today, seeing a distorted and embroidered version of a practice which was at one time very common not only in Britain, but across many parts of Europe. Indeed, it lingers on to this day, handed down over thousands of years.

Chapter 3

Echoes of the Past

Before embarking upon the subject of this chapter, which is the idea that images from the past, together with specific incidents and even the character of particular individuals, can be preserved by word of mouth for centuries or millennia, it might be interesting to look at one case of this happening, one about which we can be very sure. This is necessary, for otherwise the thesis of this whole book, that our images of wizards and witches are actually folk memories handed down from long ago, may appear to be built on sand.

For 400 or 500 years after the Trojan War, traditions about the events in that conflict were handed down orally. Then, around the eighth century BC, they were put into the form of an epic poem by a man we know as Homer. It was another century or two before this was all written down. In short, for something like 600 years, everything about the siege of Troy relied upon the memories of those who took part in it and their ability to tell others, who in turn repeated what they had heard to their children and so on. Imagine if the only knowledge we had of the Battle of Agincourt had been handed down to us by word of mouth from those who took part. You might expect that between the battle itself in 1415 and the present day, every genuine detail would have become either hopelessly distorted or altogether lost and nothing useful would remain in these garbled old legends, other than a tiny kernel of accuracy, perhaps simply that there was fighting between English and French soldiers. Even that might be open to doubt and people centuries later might not even be sure whether the Battle of Agincourt even took place at all or was just an invented story about the friction between England and France.

Until the nineteenth century, this is how most people thought of the Trojan War, as something dreamed up by a poet. There were so many fantastic bits in it about gods coming down to earth disguised as men, that many scholars disregarded the whole of the *Iliad* as a work of the imagination. Today, we know differently. Patient archaeological excavations and studies of the original text show that the geography of the area around the city of Troy matches fairly precisely an actual location in Asia Minor, the area which we now call Turkey. One detail from the *Iliad* was confirmed in the most surprising and unexpected way. Book 10 of the *Iliad* contains the following lines;

> Meriones gave Odysseus a bow, a quiver and a sword, and put a cleverly made leather helmet on his head. On the inside there was a strong lining on interwoven straps, onto which a felt cap had been sewn in. The outside was cleverly adorned all around with rows of white tusks from a shiny-toothed boar, the tusks running in alternate directions in each row.

This helmet sounded like something dreamed up by a poet! Whoever could imagine protective headgear made of boars' tusks?

With the beginning of careful and systematic archaeology in the nineteenth century, a series of strange discoveries were made in the areas which fell under the sway of the ancient Greeks. Not only were monumental carvings found showing warriors with odd helmets covered in curved ridges, but also actual examples of helmets made of boars' tusks; precisely as Homer relates. All these date from centuries before the writing of the *Iliad* and show how the oral tradition kept alive a trifling detail of the weaponry of the Trojan War.

Oral memories relating to weapons certainly linger on for centuries, but those connected with religion can last for not hundreds, but thousands of years. The world at which we looked in Chapter 1, that of Bronze Age Europe, faded away 3,000 years ago, but a substantial proportion of the population in Britain and many other countries still follow at least one of the religious practices of this long-vanished society. In short, a fifth of people in the United Kingdom adhere to a practice sanctioned and endorsed by the wizards who wore pointed hats and advised on correct behaviour 4,000 years ago! Before looking at this though, let's think about something utterly mundane, our children's school holidays. This is one way in which we observe traditions from the way of life which existed in Europe over 5,000 years ago, the time of the Stone Age. It is no exaggeration to say that for the average family, whatever religion they follow or wherever their origin, the rhythm of Stone Age life rules their whole lives in Europe and North America. Thinking about this will prepare us for the idea that we are still very much affected by the belief-system of people who lived around 4,000 BC.

Here is a simple question, which most people with children at school have never troubled to ask themselves. Why is it that round the time of the Winter Solstice and the Spring Equinox they have to start thinking about childcare, because their children's schools close down for a few weeks at this time of year? And why should the longest holiday of the school year coincide with the Celtic festival of Lugnasad, the traditional start of the harvest season? These seem, on the face of it, ridiculous questions. Why, you may as well ask the reason that in Britain the autumn half-term holiday always seems to coincide with the Celtic Samhain festival and the first half-term holiday of the year to fall on Imbolc. Of course, there are school holidays at Christmas and Easter. The truth is that the festival held around the time of the Winter Solstice has nothing to do with Christmas, there being not the least reason to suppose that the founder of the Christian religion was born at that time of year. This was a time of feasting long before the Christian missionaries arrived in Europe. The Romans marked the time near the shortest day of the year with gluttony and drunkenness and so too did the uncivilized tribes in northern Europe. That this was a sacred time of year and has been so in Europe for at least 5,000 years can easily be seen by looking at some very old monuments and tombs.

The passage tomb of Newgrange, in Ireland's County Meath, was built 3,000 years before the birth of Jesus, which we now celebrate in mid-winter. At Newgrange, the rising sun at dawn on the day of the Winter Solstice shines directly down a narrow passage and illuminates the heart of the tomb. When it was constructed, the Winter Solstice must have been of tremendous significance to the men who planned Newgrange. They were obviously not thinking about the Christmas holidays!

Religion of any sort is less important to the people of Europe than was once the case, but they nevertheless preserve a special cycle which has no connection to Christianity, Islam or any other modern religion. This sequence is based not upon the birth or death of this or that religious leader, but instead upon the progress of the sun on its journey across the heavens. The course of this celestial movement was taught to them by their wizards. The year was at that time, and still is, although we never talk about it, divided not into twelve parts, but eight. The longest and shortest days, which we now call the solstices, those of equal length, the equinoxes, and then the mid points between these four days. This cycle provides the foundation for the lives of everybody in Europe and so forms the basis for the timing of the school holidays.

In the United States, people have a quaint tradition called Groundhog Day, about which some readers may have heard. The idea is to predict the future by examining the shadows of small mammals. Groundhog Day falls on 2 February, which also happens to be both the Feast of the Purification of the Virgin Mary and the Celtic festival of Imbolc too. All fall on the day midway between the Winter Solstice and the Spring Equinox. It is also of course when the schools in Britain have a half-term holiday.

The old calendar is a fascinating topic and we have done no more than skim the surface; more information may be found in the appendix to this book, 'The Magical Year'. Enough has perhaps been said though to show that a cycle of celebration and observance which was already old 5,000 years ago is sedulously adhered to today by everybody in Europe, even if they are unaware why they follow this series of holidays and holy days. It is a relic of the distant past, so deeply embedded in our day-to-day lives that we scarcely notice it. The very same thing is true of our perceptions of wizards, witches and fairies. The information which we all possess about such matters, as part of our cultural heritage, is buried so deeply in our subconscious minds that we are not even aware of it. We love the Narnia books, but don't know why. The film *Maleficent* strikes a chord within us, but not on any conscious level. Let us delve into our past a little and see why we feel as we do and how this in turn affects our behaviour and thought processes.

To understand the world in which European shamans or wizards arose, it is necessary to appreciate that there existed no clear demarcation in prehistoric times between the world of the living and that of the dead, or between the world of mortal men and the realm of the gods. These various worlds intersected at special places, most particularly in rivers, lakes and caves. There was also no real division between everyday life and religion. Today, we have houses and streets, shops and factories, football stadium and parks, all of which make up the practical world of real life. There are also little corners of the world, shut off from us by walls, which are concerned with sacrifice and the worship of the Deity. These are churches and mosques, temples and synagogues. They are quite separate from day-to-day life. It was not always so.

Today, a project such as building a bridge, pier or jetty has no spiritual dimension; it is something concerned with our material world. Three or four thousand years ago, an enterprise of that sort would have been bound up with what might be termed spiritual matters. In 1993, the remains of a wooden pier were excavated on the bank of the River Thames in London. Stout posts were found at very low tide to be protruding from the mud and leading from the bank at Vauxhall to towards the centre of the river. The wood was carbon-dated to around 1500 BC. At first, it was assumed that this was the first bridge across the Thames, but two things altered that view of the case. First, it appeared to stop just a short distance from the riverbank, rather than extending to the opposite bank, and secondly two bronze spearheads were discovered near the piles which formed the structure. These had not been accidentally lost, but had rather been driven deep into the ground near the posts, deliberately disposed of in this way.

It should be mentioned that many fine examples of Iron Age and Bronze Age weaponry have been fished out of the Thames. The horned helmet seen in Illustration 6 is one such item. Since these things were exceedingly valuable, it is very unlikely that they were simply misplaced or carelessly dropped in the water. If such a mishap had occurred, then the most strenuous efforts would have been made to recover them. It is more likely that they were deliberately thrown into the water as sacrifices. On the north side of Lake Neuchâtel in Switzerland is the village of La Tène. This location has given its name to an entire Iron Age culture. The reason for this was that during a drought in 1857 the level of the lake fell dramatically and revealed many swords and shield bosses, along with a great quantity of jewellery. There were also wooden posts, like those later found in London. These formed part of a short pier, which led out towards the middle of the lake. A curious circumstance was that the swords showed no sign of wear. They had seemingly been thrown into the water from the jetty or pier, brand-new, just as they had been made.

At Flag Fen, near the English city of Peterborough, a similar structure was found, consisting of thousands of wooden posts leading to a platform over the water. Just as in London and at La Tène, many bronze objects have been recovered. Both La Tène and Flag Fen are part of the same ritual as was probably practised at what is now Vauxhall.

Those wishing to demonstrate their unswerving devotion to the gods or respect for the dead, perhaps sometimes to expiate a sin, would visit one of these piers. Very likely, these would be impressive occasions, with crowds gathering to watch what was to happen. The whole affair would be arranged and supervised by a wizard or priest, ensuring that the correct incantations or spells were said. Then a colossally expensive sword, shield or helmet, perhaps made specially for the occasion, would be hurled out into the deepest part of the river or lake, where it would be impossible to retrieve it. These swords and so on would be shiny and new, not as they are now in museum cases, coated with a dull patina of oxidization. It is little wonder that such extraordinary exhibitions should have been talked about and the story of them passed down through the generations. It is a garbled version of such stories which has been preserved in the story of the Lady of the Lake and the wonderful sword being thrown into the water.

But, readers may be thinking at this point, surely this is all just an historical curiosity, with no conceivable relevance to the modern world and only the flimsiest and most tenuous connection to wizardry and fairies? Not a bit of it! The practice of Bronze Age and Iron Age peoples in Europe of hurling precious swords into bodies of water is still very much alive, albeit in a slightly modified form, and Merlin the wizard looms over the story of Excalibur. Something which a fifth of the population in Britain do regularly provides us with a direct link to the story of Excalibur, the sword of King Arthur at which we have looked.

We looked briefly at the Arthurian tale of the Lady of the Lake and speculated that it might have its origins in the sacrificial offerings of swords made so extensively in Bronze Age Europe. Rivers, lakes and wells were all popular sites for depositions of this kind and there are two possible explanations for the custom. One is that the swords, shields, helmets and cauldrons were being offered up to some local deity. It also possible that they were being given to the dead, as a way of gaining favour with ancestors or perhaps dead strangers who might be minded to cause harm. Pools, springs and wells were sometimes believed to be entrances to the underworld, the land of the dead. Excavated Roman wells in London, as well as lakes in wales like Llyn Fawr, all show how widespread this practice was. Encouraged by religious beliefs of the time, as transmitted to them by their shamans or wizards, Bronze Age men and women often committed valuable metal goods to sources of water in this way. Incredibly, the practice continues to this very day.

In November 2006 a financial marketing agency compiled a report called the 'Fountain Money Mountain'. They found that one person in five in Britain regularly throws coins into fountains, wells and other watery locations. This will probably come as no surprise to most readers; after all, it's what people tend to do near small bodies of water, isn't it? In London, the fountains in Trafalgar Square and at Marble Arch accumulate coins thrown in for luck. Those designing public fountains and pools take it for granted that passers-by will toss in coins. This is all so obvious, that it scarcely needs to be mentioned. The question we pose though is why it should be regarded as such a natural and inevitable state of affairs. Where do people pick up this habit of tossing coins into water?

Between 3,000 and 4,000 years ago, the act of sacrificing a treasured sword to either the gods or to the spirits of the dead was a grand affair, presided over by a wizard. As the years passed though, gifts to the other world became more commonplace. The presence of a religious leader was no longer required and instead of an expensive sword, old or broken weapons would be thrown instead into the water. By the time the Romans occupied Britain, from 43 AD onwards, the sacrifices were purely nominal. Broken knives were more common than swords and many people gave a cash equivalent instead, just a coin or two as a token gesture. In this way what was once a major religious ceremony degenerates into mere superstition.

It is now easy enough to see how the modern custom of throwing coins into pools and fountains arose. Most of us who do this acquired the habit from our parents. Perhaps they gave us a penny and told us to throw it in and make a wish. We then pass this quaint action on to our own children. Sometimes, instead of making a specific wish, the coin is thrown in just 'for luck'. That this little bit of everyday life, indulged in regularly by 20 per cent of the British population has a direct connection with Excalibur and the Lady of the Lake is perhaps not as widely known as it might be.

A grander and more spectacular modern example of making such sacrifices to the gods and goddesses of the water takes place when a large ocean-going vessel is launched. Before a warship, submarine or cruise liner slides into the water for the first time, a bottle of some expensive alcoholic beverage is broken open, as a means of propitiating the spirits of the water and asking them to look favourably upon the ship when once it sails the seas.

It is not only to the minor deities living in the water to whom we still make our offerings. Sometimes, in just the same way, we send our charity to the world of the dead. This too is part of the same, ancient tradition which was established by Bronze Age wizards and shamans and has, over the course of thousands of years, become so ingrained in us that it is now practically second nature. A perfect example of this may be seen today in London's Southwark Cathedral, just a stone's throw from that great symbol of modernity, the office block known as the Shard.

In 1977, excavations at the cathedral led to the discovery of a well, into which had been thrown statues of gods and pieces of an altar. Some while later, the remains of a Roman road were found, deep below the present ground level upon which the Cathedral stands. At the same time that this was found, an empty medieval stone coffin was also unearthed. During the building of a new centre, these two features were left as they were and a 15ft deep shaft left open, so that they could be seen by visitors. Almost at once, the tribute of coins began. The target was the stone coffin. Despite notices being placed at the site, requesting people not to throw coins, for fear of damaging the old sarcophagus, people still could not resist. The symbolism of the shaft leading down below ground level and the empty coffin proved irresistible. Those tossing coins must surely have felt that in some primeval way, they were sending offerings down to the world of the dead. Little wonder that the staff at a Christian place of worship should be irritated at such a thing. Illustration 8 shows this scene in the cathedral.

Merlin, the most famous wizard of them all, gives us another good starting point when looking at folk memories and how far back they may stretch. His significance does not begin and end with his ability to cast spells. Just as Gandalf is for many people the most loved character from *The Lord of the Rings*, so too is Merlin more popular and better known than most of the other people who feature in the myths about the court of King Arthur. The solitary wizard motif is a powerful one.

Legends about Merlin were swirling around in Wales before the Norman Conquest of 1066, but it was not until around 1139 that a Welshman called Geoffrey of Monmouth set down information about him in his monumental work *History of the Kings of Britain.* Although he claimed to have been consulting an ancient manuscript in writing his history, Geoffrey of Monmouth, who later became a bishop, was almost certainly just collecting old stories locally and then supplementing them from his own vivid imagination. It has been suggested that Merlin was based upon a real person in the sixth century AD, who aided in the defence of England against the Saxons who invaded the country after the withdrawal of the Roman legions at the beginning of the fifth century AD. The truth is almost certainly far more interesting than this. The wizard Merlin is perhaps a folk memory of someone who actually lived thousands of years earlier, at the time that Stonehenge was being built.

Although our ideas about Merlin have been embellished over the years by various poets and writers, most notably Sir Thomas Mallory in the fifteenth century and Alfred Lord Tennyson in the nineteenth century, the picture painted by Geoffrey of Monmouth provides the earliest image of the wizard; gleaned as it probably was from folk stories handed down across the generations. Merlin was, according to this first version, an adviser to kings and also a seer. Most of what he accomplished though was done by ordinary human means; he was a great prophet and thinker, but his magical abilities were vague and less important.

One very curious anecdote which found its way into *History of the Kings of Britain* concerns the construction of Stonehenge. The stones of Stonehenge, according to Geoffrey of Monmouth, were originally part of a stone circle in another part of the British Isles and were dug up from there by means of ropes and pulleys, loaded onto ships and brought, part of the way by sea, to their present position on Salisbury Plain. Merlin was the architect of this enterprise and no magic was involved, just a great deal of ingenuity and manpower.

On the fact of it, this sounds a ridiculous and far-fetched story, but a recent archaeological discovery has caused historians to re-examine the account and it is now thought that there may well be something in it. Geoffrey of Monmouth said that Merlin told King Aurelius,

> If you are desirous to honour the burying-place of these men with an everlasting monument, send for the Giant's Dance, which is in Killaraus, a mountain in Ireland. For there is a structure of stones there, which none of this age could raise, without a profound knowledge of the mechanical arts. They are stones of a vast magnitude and wonderful quality; and if they can be placed here, as they are there, round this spot of ground, they will stand for ever.

It has been known for over a century that the original stones used to construct the first version of Stonehenge came from a long way away from Salisbury Plain, where Stonehenge now stands. These are the so-called bluestones and they come from Pembrokeshire in South Wales. It has also been suggested that these blocks of stone, which were set up at Stonehenge around 3000 BC, might have been transported by sea for part of the way. This could conceivably tie in with the story which Geoffrey of Monmouth tells about the stones being carried by ship, although some kind of raft would be more likely. What about the idea though that the stones which were set up to form Stonehenge were at one time part of another stone circle? This sounded a little unlikely, but archaeological research in the last few years has confirmed that this is precisely what did happen.

The quarry from which the first stones placed at Stonehenge were taken was identified a long time ago as being 140 miles away in the Preseli Hills of Wales. Excavations there in 2008 uncovered evidence of Stone Age work at the site. The only difficulty was that this was carbon dated to 3400 BC, about 400 years before construction of Stonehenge began. Surely it could not have taken 400 years to transport the stones to Wiltshire? Even less probably was that after the stones had been hewn from the rocky outcrop, they were simply left to lie about for centuries. What had happened to those large stones, each one weighing between two and four tons, before they were taken to Salisbury Plain?

Three miles from the area where the bluestones had been quarried is a prehistoric site called Waun Mawn, where four megaliths are to be found, only one of which is still standing. Archaeological examination of the surrounding area showed that a stone circle once stood there, with a diameter of 110m, exactly the same width as the bank surrounding Stonehenge. Digging led to the finding of holes where stones had once been erected in a ring. Using thermoluminescence, which can show how long since soil has been exposed to sunlight, the researchers were able to fix the date of the removal of the stones of Waun Mawn to around 3000 BC. The question was settled conclusively when the base of one of the excavated holes which had held a bluestone were found to match one of the stones at Stonehenge 'like a lock and key', as an archaeologist put it.

The implications of all this are quite staggering. The story about Stonehenge having been built from stones which had previously formed part of another stone circle many miles away was first written down in the twelfth century AD by Geoffrey of Monmouth. He had picked up the story from Welsh folklore or oral tradition. This means that the story of the bluestones must have been passed down by word of mouth for some 4,000 years before it was recorded in written form.

Merlin is the archetypal wizard and to find a legend linked to his name and dating back 5,000 years is of interest, because it hints at a connection with the Neolithic world on the cusp of the Bronze Age, a time when the strange world at which we looked in Chapter 1 had its origin. It may sound unlikely, but most of us are still influenced by the religious practices and magical ideas of that time, which linger on in our lives and have the effect of giving us a faint memory of that ancient time. To see how this works, let us look at another wizard from thousands of years ago, one who became in effect deified after his death. We are all of us familiar with this semi-divine shaman, because we still come across his name every single week.

The day of the week Wednesday is a corruption of 'Woden's Day'. Woden was the chief god of northern Germany and Scandinavia in the years following the collapse of the Roman Empire, but before the conquest of Europe by the Romans was widely known across the entire continent. Woden, or Odin as he is better known, was in the habit of walking the earth in the guise of an old man with a staff. His appearance, according to old Norse *Eddas,* was almost indistinguishable from that of Gandalf. He carried a staff, wore a long cloak and on his head had a pointed hat. Sometimes, instead of a hat he had a hood pulled down over his face.

We shall be looking further at Odin later, but for now it is enough to know that he supposedly had only one eye and wore the floppy hat or hood to conceal this fact, in case people he met guessed his identity. Images of Odin, first a wizard and later a god, have been found in England and carbon-dated to 2,300 BC. This subject will be explored in detail in a later chapter. A thousand years ago, children in Scandinavia used to put straw in their shoes when they went to bed at about the time of the Winter Solstice, in the middle of December. They did this because Odin was known, among other titles, as Father Yule. It was said that if children put the straw out for his horse Sleipnir, then in the morning they would find their shoes filled with sweets or little gifts.

It is likely that readers will by now have seen the similarities in an old man with a hood called Father Yule who arrived in the middle of December to bring gifts to children. The custom of leaving out straw for Father Yule's horse has of course mutated over the years to leaving out carrots for his reindeer and perhaps a mince pie for the man himself. It will help at this point if readers ask themselves why it is that in some families to this day, children put out food for Father Christmas's reindeers in this way. No parent has learned about this tradition from a book and decided to follow it. It is one of those things which has been passed down through families purely by word of mouth. The parents who carry out this practice for their children do so because their own parents did so when they were themselves small. This is a ritual which has been preserved as a folk memory dating back many centuries. It is another window on the past. On the night when children expect a hooded old man to visit their home in a magic chariot or sleigh drawn by his cult animals, we encourage them to anticipate this visit by putting out food for the wizard and his beasts.

If, as seems highly likely, Odin or Woden has been an important figure in European myth for over 4,000 years, then our harmless little ritual of putting out provender for the beasts who draw him along may well be a survival from the Bronze Age. Nor is it the only practice in which we still engage which may have its roots so far in the distant past.

We looked earlier at the subject of water-spirits and their lingering attraction even in this age of science. One last anecdote about such matters might be of interest. One of the most beloved of fairy stories and one which many parents delight to tell their children is the story of the three Billy Goats Gruff. Through the language used in the Scandinavian version and the internal structure, the story of the Billy Goats Gruff and the troll is evidently at least a thousand years old. It tells of the flip side of asking the spirits of the water for help and shows what happens to those who do not treat them with respect and make the due offerings. The goats in the story simply cross over the water without so much as a by-your-leave and certainly do not regard the guardian of the bridge as being worth propitiating. The fierce spirit then tries to exact retribution.

We have looked at two rituals, both commonly undertaken in Britain and mainland Europe which have been handed down, by word of mouth, for many years, most likely for thousands of years. Casting money into pools of water and leaving out carrots for the cult beasts of a mythical and semi-divine being are both still extant in the twenty-first century. These practices are associated with the gods who were once worshipped before the coming of Christianity. This ties in with the theme of this book, which is the search for the origin of our ideas about wizards, witches and fairies. The role of wizards was, during their first appearance in Britain, indistinguishable at times from that of priests. They were guardians of knowledge and guided ordinary people in their understanding of the nature of the gods and how they must be served and propitiated. Odin or Woden, chief of these gods, often adopted the guise of a wizard and may originally have been one before he was elevated in the minds of his followers to divine status.

The assertion has been made that things such as sacrificing coins to fountains, wells and pools can tell us something about Bronze Age Europe and the way of life which existed at that time. In this chapter and the preceding ones we have looked at the heritage of a particular time in Europe's history. We have seen that our ideas about all manner of things from favourite Victorian novels to modern television programmes might have originated at this time. Mention has been made of the Indo-Europeans and their culture. It is time now to delve deep into the past and try to reconstruct the world, or at least one corner of it, as it was 5,000 years ago. In short, it is time to meet our ancestors, the Yamnaya.

Chapter 4

The Coming of the Yamnaya

In the late eighteenth century, some scholars noticed that Sanskrit, the ancient language of India, bore a remarkable and unmistakable similarity to both Latin and Greek. It is also possible to recognize the derivation of some Sanskrit words by comparing them with English equivalents. To give a simple example, the Hindu god of fire is called Agni. This is similar to the Latin 'ignis' and also cognate with the modern English words 'igneous' and 'ignite'; both of which are associated with burning and heat. In Sanskrit 'mother' is 'matar', whereas in Latin and Greek it is 'mater'. The English word 'maternal' comes from the same root. It requires no great stretch of the imagination nor extensive knowledge of etymology to deduce that in some earlier language, common to Sanskrit, Latin, Greek and English, there was once a word relating to fire which had the consonants 'G' and 'N' in it. Nor is it difficult to imagine that the words for 'mother' in those languages all began with the letter 'M'.

In 1786 William Jones, a scholar of ancient languages who was at that time the Chief Justice of India, wrote that:

> The Sanskrit language, whatever may be its antiquity, is of wonderful structure; more perfect than the Greek, more copious than the Latin, and more exquisitely refined than either; yet bearing to both of them a stronger affinity, both in the roots of verbs and in the forms of grammar, than could have been produced by accident; so strong that no philologer could examine all the three without believing them to have sprung from some common source, which, perhaps, no longer exists.

Sanskrit, the ancient language in which the earliest Hindu scriptures are written, was a product of Proto-Indo-European, as were Latin and Greek. In fact almost all the languages of Europe and Northern India, together with Iranian, are ultimately derived from this tongue. We know this because of the great similarities between distantly-separated languages. Lithuanian, one of the languages spoken in the Baltic region of Northern Europe, is so similar to early forms of Indian languages that it was said in the nineteenth century that a Lithuanian peasant living in a remote and isolated village would probably have been able to communicate with a Brahmin priest who spoke Sanskrit. In Sanskrit 'sheep' is 'avis', as it is also in Lithuanian. 'Fire' is 'agnis' in Sanskrit and 'ugnis' in Lithuanian. The word 'son' is 'sunus' in both languages.

The Brothers Grimm are famous today for their collecting of fairy tales from across the whole of Europe. It was only possible for them to do so because they were proficient in various languages. Once the theory was advanced that many Indian languages shared a common origin with those of Europe, Jakob and Wilhelm Grimm worked out, by comparing words from various languages ancient and modern, the rules by which those languages evolved and developed over the centuries. The race was on, firstly to reconstruct this mother tongue and then to find from where these 'Indo-Europeans', those who had spoken this language, had come; where their homeland had been. These twin tasks turned out to be inextricably linked, because once certain words had been identified as having been part of the vocabulary of the first Indo-Europeans, as they were provisionally named, this would shed light upon the environment in which they lived.

Some of the words in the original language from which most European languages and many in India are descended are interesting, but tell us little about the society which used them. The English word 'water', for instance, is similar in some other languages. It is 'wasser' in German and 'voda' in Russian. The further back we look, the closer we get to the original word from which these are derived. Uriah the Hittite, from the Biblical story of King David, would have used the word 'watar'. This was around 3,000 years ago. All these words come from an original word for water which was 'wodar'. This is all very interesting, some readers may think, but we seem to be veering off the topic of this book, which is about how our ideas of wizards, witches and fairies arose. I must crave indulgence for a little, until the connection is made plain.

We know from the words which have been reconstructed of the language spoken by the first Indo-Europeans, a language which is sometimes called Proto-Indo-European, or PIE for short, that these people had domesticated animals. They knew the 'gwou' or cow from which they obtained 'melg'. They used 'uksen' to plough fields and pull wagons. We know they wove cloth because the English word 'weave' and other words in European and Indian languages all come from an original 'webh'. They had a word for copper, but not iron, which strongly suggests that this was a Bronze Age people, limiting the time at which they might have flourished. Studying the language gives us hints too about where this tribe once lived.

Those first Indo-Europeans had a word for snow, which was 'sneighw'. We can see this in our own 'snow', the Russian 'sneig' and also the French 'neige'. This probably rules out India or the Middle East as the homeland, although of course snow is occasionally seen in countries such as Israel and Syria. They had no word for 'sea' or 'ocean', but a word for little rivers, which was 'strew' and also a word for ponds. There were snakes where they lived, 'serp', from which of course the English word 'serpent' comes. There was also an animal which the called the 'bhebhru', which we know today as the beaver. Combining this with one or two other clues, such as the fact that the people who spoke this language were familiar with both beech trees and birches, suggests a homeland in northern Europe.

The changes in pronunciation, which Jacob and Wilhelm Grimm discovered, followed what became known as Grimm's Law, after the folklorists, and occurred at a certain speed. Because of this, it is believed today that what is now known as Proto-Indo-European was being spoken some 5,000 or 6,000 years ago, before it began to split into the many different languages which are now spoken in India and Europe.

There was until relatively recently fierce debate about the original homeland of the people whom we know as the Indo-Europeans, but with new studies of DNA, the question is more or less settled. Five thousand years ago in the grassy plains of what is now Ukraine, southern Russia and Kazakhstan there lived a large group of tribes. These people were pastoralists, which is to say they kept livestock which they allowed to roam freely. We know how these people lived and about some of their beliefs, not from archaeological evidence but rather from tracing back words from European and Indian languages and seeing if they might have had a common origin in the language of what are known as the Yamnaya people of the steppes. A few shrewd guesses are then necessary to complete the picture. This all sounds a good deal more complicated than is actually the case and the best way to make the matter clear is by giving an example. Before doing this, perhaps we need to see why we call these people the Yamnaya, which was not their own name for themselves.

The people who lived in those broad, grassy plains so many thousands of years ago used to bury some of their dead in pit graves, covered with mounds of earth. The Russian word for 'relating to pits' is 'Yamnaya', which has become the name by which this culture is generally known. We know something of the Yamnaya from what they buried in their graves. The bones of sheep, cattle and horses are found there, for instance, together with wooden carts or wagons. Pieces of gear for riding horses have also been found. These people were on the cusp of the Bronze Age, because although they used flint arrowheads, the working of copper was beginning to spread, as well as the making of that alloy of copper and tin which we call bronze. This of course ties in perfectly with what can already be deduced from the study of their reconstructed language.

The Yamnaya were nomadic pastoralists, which is to say that they moved from place to place as their flocks and herds stripped an area of enough scrubby grass to satisfy them. Perhaps a good modern parallel would be the Bedouin of the Middle East who pursue a similar lifestyle. They pitch their tents in a certain place and allow their goats to wander around, gaining what sustenance they may. Children often act as shepherds or goatherds. When one place is denuded of vegetation, the Bedouin pack up their tents and move on. They use camels as beasts of burden to carry their food, water and tents, but the Yamnaya used heavy wagons with solid wheels. Such a wagon, when fully laden, would have been far too heavy for a horse to pull and so oxen would have hauled them across the steppes.

The Yamnaya did not arise spontaneously; they succeeded other cultures in the same general area. Recent DNA analysis indicates that they were the descents of hunter-gatherers from Eastern Europe and the Middle East. This is intriguing, because it allows us to trace back Yamnaya ideas about wizards to the area from which they originally came, which was Europe during the last Ice Age. For about a thousand years the Yamnaya culture flourished in a very wide geographical area. North of the Black Sea and Caspian Sea, they occupied an area larger than Spain, France and Germany put together and beyond their territory, the limitless grasslands stretched away in all directions, seemingly to infinity. If they needed more room for grazing their flocks and herds, then they simply moved north, south, east or west as the spirit took them. They needed a lot of space because their oxen and sheep needed plenty of grass to graze on and each tribe was constantly on the move in search of new pastures for their animals.

What is hypothesized is that around 3500 or 3000 BC the Yamnaya people, whom we might just as well call the Indo-Europeans, began leaving their homeland and moving south and west. Why they should have begun these migrations is not clear. It has been suggested that climate change might be implicated and that the steppe was becoming drier and more arid. Equally likely is that the constant grazing of oxen and sheep made it harder and harder to find places verdant enough for the herds to flourish. This is seen with the Bedouin who are mentioned above. Some of the desert areas of the Middle East have been attributed, at least in part, to the rapacity of the goats which accompany the Bedouin on their wanderings. These factors, combined perhaps with a growing population, led to pressures which resulted for the Yamnaya in a drive away from their familiar lands and into the unknown. They took with them not only their language but also their customs and, of interest to us, their belief system.

In the west, the continent into which the Yamnaya expanded was very different from the grassy plains from which they came. For one thing, much of Europe was heavily forested at this time, with fairly small areas cleared for space to build villages and farms. It was an eerie landscape which they encountered because the communities who lived there believed that the land upon which they lived was itself sacred and belonged as much to the gods and the spirits of the dead as it did to them. They shared their communities with unseen powers and this was reflected in some of the structures which they erected. All this was very new for the Yamnaya, who were of course used to moving from place to place, rather than regarding any particular fixed location on the earth as being of great significance. One might say that they took their gods with them as they travelled.

A specific example of how strongly attached the Europeans of that time, whom the Yamnaya encountered, were to particular spots on their territory might help us to understand how deep ran the attachment of those in Europe for their land. The earth itself, hills, valley and streams, was seen as being a holy thing, but it could be enhanced with permanent additions constructed by the people living on it. This idea, that the land around them was sacred, is known today as the 'ritual landscape'. The devotion to certain places could be unbelievably intense and long-lasting. We are all familiar with Stonehenge, which was built on a part of Salisbury Plain which for some reason was very special at that time. The digging of the circular bank which would become Stonehenge began about 3000 BC. The earliest monuments in that area though were discovered during the building of a car park for those visiting the monument. Three post-holes were found, in which huge wooden poles like the totem poles of the Native Americans were once placed. These holes had been dug in 8500 BC, 5,500 years before Stonehenge was begun. That is some considerable attachment to a particular spot.

It was very settled communities of this kind, which were passionately in tune with the landscape in which they lived, that the Yamnaya found when they arrived in western Europe. For the newcomers, this was all very strange. They themselves were modern people. They used metal weapons and tools, while the people of Europe were still using flint-tipped arrows and spears, they had domesticated animals such as oxen and horses, they had mastered the use of the wheel. They probably saw themselves as the future, as they trundled along through stretches of land which had a deep connection with those living on it going back over 5,000 years.

Of course, it is unlikely that the folk who were driving west towards the Atlantic had any words equivalent to 'colonialism' or 'genocide', but that is what their conquests amount to, especially when they reached Britain between 4,500 and 5,000 years ago. Whether through deliberate slaughter or by the importation of diseases against which those living on the island had no defence, the descendants of the Yamnaya replaced the native population, until only scattered remnants were to be found, hiding in remote haunts in mountains and forests.

Because they were nomads, the earthworks, standing stones, ditches and banks and so on which covered parts of the country such as what is now Wiltshire would have been viewed with awe. They had always been essentially wanderers and had been so even before leaving their homeland. For this reason, the Yamnaya had never built anything larger or more complex than an earth mound over a grave. Here though were monuments such as standing stones and huge earthworks like Silbury Hill. This artificial hill in Wiltshire, which looms 40m high over the surrounding plain, is an astonishing enough sight today. What the Yamnaya made of it can only be imagined. Even more bizarre to them must have been what are known today as causewayed enclosures. These are huge circles of ditches and banks, with entrances left like bridges across the ditch; these causeways gave their name to these structures. We know that people gathered there to eat, but whether these were like marketplaces or town squares, simply somewhere to socialise, is completely unknown. Some of these enclosures certainly had a ritual use; human bones have been found buried in the ditches which surround them. They are mixed with animal bones, which suggests that feasting took place there as well.

The causewayed enclosures might very possibly have had a nightmarish quality about them when the invaders arrived. Like almost every human culture, starting with the Neanderthals of the Middle East, the Yamnaya disposed of their dead by burial. This was the neatest and most hygienic way of dealing with a corpse, respecting also the sensitivities of the dead person's family. The Neolithic farmers of Britain had, as far as the evidence can be gauged, a different way of treating the dead bodies of their tribe. This was by excarnation. In India, the Parsees place dead bodies in tall structures called Towers of Silence, There, they are exposed to the birds of the air; scavengers and raptors. Only when the corpse has been completely picked clean and reduced to a sun-bleached skeleton is it buried.

It seems likely that the people of Britain 5,000 years ago had very similar customs to the Parsees, in that skeletons recovered from such sites show signs of having been pecked by birds and gnawed by animals, something unlikely to have happened had they been buried soon after death. These were not lone travellers who died far from home, but rather the remains of human corpses which had been systematically cleaned of flesh. The bones were buried in the ditches of the causewayed enclosures. Combined with the remains of food and animal bones recovered from the same locations, a disturbing possibility is raised. This is that the corpses of the tribe would be exposed in these places to be excarnated or stripped of their flesh by scavengers and insects and that even while this process was taking place, people were coming there to hold feasts. It has been suggested that perhaps relatives came to have picnics and share their food with the dead. This is because in some such enclosures holes have been deliberately dug and offerings of food deposited in them.

The Yamnaya, who disposed of corpses quickly in the traditional way, might have been appalled to come across a sanctuary in which human remains and the detritus of feasting lay mingled together. Perhaps they thought that they had come across the remains of cannibalistic orgies of something of the kind. It is even possible that the old fairy tales such as *Jack and the Beanstalk*, which feature ogres, might have been inspired by these ghastly places. Everything about the lands into which they were venturing over 4,000 years ago must have seemed strange and disconcerting to the Yamnaya; very different indeed from the open plains upon which their people had lived for thousands of years.

Within a few centuries, the old life in Britain had ended and the day of the Indo-Europeans had begun. The languages which had been spoken in Europe since the end of the last Ice Age had become extinct and, with one or two notable exceptions such as the Basques of present-day France and Spain, only Indo-European dialects and languages would be spoken from now on. It was this transformed continent which formed the backdrop to all the heroic tales which we know today, from *Jack and the Beanstalk* to *Game of Thrones*. What did this world of wizards and magic, heroes and fairies, look like?

There were no nation-states in that Europe of 3,000–4,000 years ago. Here and there might be an especially strong chieftain of the invading tribes who might have fancied himself to be a king and established a realm, but it is doubtful if his writ ran further than the area of a modern English county. Although forests still covered much of the land, there were many cleared areas where villages stood, surrounded by cultivated fields. The society, such as it was, of the new settlers was divided roughly into three categories. This tripartite division has had a great effect on the culture of Europe since that time and it is there that we first find embodied the idea of wizards as a separate and distinct class.

The Coming of the Yamnaya   49

Before looking at the division of Indo-European society into three classes, it might be interesting and relevant to the subject in hand to consider the prevalence of the number three in both our own modern world and also in the very earliest fiction from Europe, which we call fairy stories. Embedded in many of those old stories is the mystical importance of the number 'three'. People are given three wishes, three attempts to undertake some tricky task, three days to solve a riddle and so on. There are three Billy Goats Gruff, three bears live in the house which Goldilocks visits; everywhere the number three crops up. Why should this be so? Why three and not eight or two?

Readers are invited to suppose that they are trying, together with another person, to lift a very heavy object. Imagine if the person with whom they were undertaking this operation said, 'Ready? On the count of four'. Or 'On the count of two'. This would strike us as being exceedingly odd. Obviously, we do things on the count of three, not two or four. Why should this be?

In everyday life, the number three is of great significance. So deeply embedded within European, and by extension American, culture is this number that we take it for granted, seldom stopping to think about what sets three apart from all other digits. We commonly say 'Third time lucky!' or initiate a synchronised action in a group of people 'On the count of three!' We sometimes voice a piece of old folklore that unlucky events tend to come in threes. There were three witches in Shakespeare's *Macbeth*, which seems very right and proper, and there were of course also three wise men. The three wise men who visited Jesus shortly after his birth are of interest, because the Bible does not specify how many there actually were. It just seems right and natural that there should have been three of them and that this how we refer to the Magi, regardless of what scripture tells us!

In the oldest fairy tales, mortals are sometimes offered three wishes. None of these fortunate men and women ever seem to have been given the chance to have five wishes granted or just two. Always, the number was three, which again sounds perfectly natural. The myths of the

Indo-Europeans, at which we shall be looking later, contain instances of people and animals which had more than one head. There was Cerberus, the three-headed dog who guarded the entrance to Hades in Greek mythology, a creature who had been inherited from the Indo-Europeans. There was too a three-headed serpent and also a three-headed ogre who featured in an Indo-European legend of cattle raiding. All such creatures had three heads and never any more or fewer.

Turning the matter over in our minds for a minute or two will reveal many other instances where the number three crops up and appears to be far more natural and appropriate than two, four or five would ever be. Without ever considering the matter, we acknowledge that this number has an almost mystic importance in our culture, although we are quite unable to say why this should be.

In the ancient world too, we see the number three appearing, especially in religious contexts. The three Fates of Greek and Roman mythology also appear as the three Norns, who performed a similar function in the Norse world. Then too, there is the manifestation of three which until fairly recently dominated the whole of the Western belief system. This is the Christian concept of the Trinity; the Father, Son and Holy Ghost. All Christian countries subscribed to this strange, triune deity and the fact that we hardly ever stop to think about what an extraordinary idea it is to worship a God composed of three separate aspects or personalities shows us how deeply ingrained is our reference for a system which relies so heavily on buses and even gods arriving in threes!

The three Norns and the three Graces were of course female, as were the Deae Matronae or Three Mothers. These appear in various guises across Europe and are regarded as manifestations of the triple nature of the Mother Goddess. Sculptures show them as women in the three typical stages of life; the virgin or maiden, the mother and the aged crone. Male deities or minor gods also appear in threes in the Romano-Celtic belief system. The slightly sinister 'Hooded Ones' are found carved on plaques at shrines in the north of England. Near Hadrian's

Wall, on the border between England and Scotland, a stone panel was unearthed showing three men wearing cloaks and hoods. These are the Genii Cucallati and their function and nature is unclear. It has been speculated that they are guardians of the underworld.

Returning for a moment to the study of language, the fact that Sanskrit and Latin had a common origin was deduced by examining both dead languages and seeing the similarities. The same method, when applied to the structure of society, reveals something very intriguing. According to the oldest legends of India, those living there were once divided into brahmanas, ksatriyas and vaisyas. Roughly translated, these are priests, warriors and herder-cultivators or farmers. This very old tradition is of course the origin of the caste system which, despite the most strenuous efforts of successive Indian governments since independence in 1948, still bedevils the country. This separation of classes which we know existed in India thousands of years ago equates very neatly with the ancient Greek arrangement of priests and magistrates, warriors and labourers and artisans. The Romans wrote of similar divisions both in their own country and also in Gaul. In Rome there were flamines, milites and quirites, while in Gaul, which occupied the area of modern-day France and Belgium, the categories were, according to Julius Caesar, druids, equites and plebes. It is here, although the fact is not immediately apparent, that we find the first written references to the wizards of Europe.

Georges Dumézil, perhaps the world's greatest expert on Indo-European culture and language, suggested that the 'priests', as they are called for short, exercised what he described as 'magico-religious' functions. That is to say that they both acted as conduits of, or mouthpieces for, the gods, but also as magicians in their own right. Sometimes they communicated the wishes of the gods, at other times they relied upon their own powers to predict the future, cast spells and similar activities.

We looked earlier at the mystical attraction of the number three and the structure of the Indo-European societies is a perfect instance of this at work. At the bottom were the farmers and labourers, above them the warriors and then, at the top of the social order, the wizards, who could sometimes act also as kings.

They had a great deal of power, because without them the farmers would be lost, not knowing when to plant grain. Wizards alone could offer advice on the correct time to plant crops and predicted such things as the Winter or Summer Solstice. They knew too the nature of the gods and how these deities could be propitiated. Some of these wizards and seers were wanderers, but others served settled communities and lived in one place. Their position was, on occasion, roughly analogous to a vicar or priest today. The men in this role sometimes wore tall, pointed hats covered with images of the moon and sun, while the women dressed in black. There is no word in modern languages which precisely denotes the functions of these people, for sometimes both men and women were seen as sorcerers and at others as priests. They even assumed the role of royalty at times.

This world was a scary and hazardous place to the people living in it. Today, the sacred and mundane are strictly separated. We have streets full of houses and shops and our religion is restricted to special buildings, usually with walls around them which symbolize their separation from day-to-day life. If ordinary people think about such matters, they tend to think that God is found in churches and possibly synagogues and mosques, but not generally in cinemas, pubs and car parks. This way of looking at the world would have seemed very strange to anybody in Europe 3,000 years ago. In those days, the gods walked the earth, generally in human guise. You literally never knew when you might bump into some old beggar and then find that he was really the king of the gods, making an impromptu inspection of humanity.

There are hints about this strange attitude in the very earliest stories of the Indo-Europeans, which are made explicit in some of the oldest written narratives. We saw in Chapter 2 that the tale of *Beauty and the Beast* had as one of the central characters a man who had fallen foul of an enchantress, fairy or witch, because he failed to recognize her true nature. The moral of that particular fable might best be summed up as, 'Do not be deceived by appearances'. Somebody who looks like an inconsequential beggar may turn out to wield enormous magical power. At least 4,000 years ago, the Indo-Europeans were familiar with this concept. It is expanded and developed in Homer's *Iliad*, in which the gods and goddesses themselves come down to earth and interfere in human affairs while disguised as mortals.

In the *Iliad*, Apollo, the sun god, adopts a number of identities, invariably of real men known to those whom he meets. Athene, the goddess of wisdom, assumes the form of an old warrior called Phoenix. This notion, of gods appearing like ordinary people, may be seen later with Odin, chief of the Norse gods, who takes the form of an old man when he wishes to see what men on earth are up to.

Apart from the risk of bumping into people who might be witches or gods under their humble outward appearance, there was also a constant threat from races other than humans. These were sometimes called dwarfs or goblins and also fairies. Nobody knew too much about them, other than that they lived in out-of-the-way places, in mountains and forests. Some of these were also thought to be masters of magic. Because they were a little in fear of these Little People, who valued their privacy and generally shunned the world of men, they were usually referred to by respectful euphemisms such as the 'good folk' or 'hidden people'.

It is in this world of shape-shifters and deceivers that we find the origins of our ideas about the nature, clothing and conduct of witches and wizards. A slight difficulty is that wizards and gods had a habit of becoming a little confused. At times, a wizard or shaman would seemingly be taken over by, or at the least become the earthly representative of, a god. At others, as we have seen, gods would present themselves as wizards or warriors. Religion and magic were so closely bound up together that it is not really possible to treat them as separate and distinct subjects. The further back in time we go, the greater the confusion, until we reach a time when men, gods and animals were all jumbled up together.

Before we explore in more detail how the wizards came to be an accepted part of society in prehistoric Europe, it is necessary to look at the practices of the hunter-gatherers who occupied Europe during the last Ice Age, which ended over 10,000 years ago. It is there that we shall find the roots of many beliefs which still affect us to this day. The Yamnaya people had their own roots at least in part in Europe, being the descendants of hunter-gatherers who had moved to the steppes many thousands of years earlier. As such, it will not be surprising to find that on their migration from Western Europe to the plains which stretch before the Urals, they carried with them some of the image and supernatural beliefs which were common in Europe at that time. Chief of these was the Horned God and the legend of the Wild Hunt.

Chapter 5

In Search of The Horned God

For a period of perhaps 12,000 years, roughly 25,000 to 13,000 years ago, the people living in Europe had to endure some of the most inhospitable climatic conditions imaginable. The northern part of the continent was completely covered in sheets of ice which stretched as far south as London. Much of the rest of Europe was like the modern tundra in the north of Russia; vast, chilly plains with sparse vegetation. In such an environment, agriculture was out of the question, even assuming that those living there had the knowledge and tools necessary to farm the land. The chief source of sustenance for the men and women living there at this time was meat and this was obtained by hunting.

In Europe today hunting, whether of foxes or deer, is a hobby. Often, as in the case of English fox hunting, it is accompanied by strange rituals, but this does not alter the fact that it is sport, rather than survival. Let's face it, nobody eats foxes. The pleasure is in the pursuit; there is no real purpose for the killing. The case could hardly have been more different 20,000 years ago. Failure to run to earth bison, deer, mammoth and other animals at that time would have meant starvation and death for entire tribes. It can scarcely be wondered at that the hunters of that time, and the communities to which they belonged, would enlist any and all help in ensuring the success of the hunt. Such help included magical spells and incantations and the men and women who claimed to know about such matters became as valued as the men who actually took part in the hunt and speared the beasts whose flesh nourished their families. Much of this supernatural aid was probably accomplished by means of what is now known as sympathetic magic. This was practised by those who may not inaptly be termed the first wizards.

Although readers may have heard of sympathetic magic, it is possible that they are not familiar with its supposed mode of operation. The expression was coined by James Frazer in his authoritative work on magic and superstition, *The Golden Bough*. Frazer defined sympathetic magic as a controlled, supernatural power designed to influence the world at a distance. He identified two forms, which he called contagion and imitation. In contagion, an object which was once in contact with something or somebody, remains connected to a scene or person forever, via mysterious forces. The imitative type of sympathetic magic entails drawing, painting or modelling a situation or living creature and so making whatever is depicted occur in real life. Another method is to act out a series of events, which will then have the effect of causing those events to take place in the real world.

A modern example of the use of sympathetic magic may be seen in homeopathy. A chemical is introduced to a container full of water, which is then shaken. Then, 90 per cent is discarded and the container filled with fresh water, which dilutes the original solution until it is a tenth as strong, and the process repeated. This might be done sixty times, until there is unlikely to be a single molecule left of the diluted chemical. However, it has in some way interacted with the water, which now bears the influence of the substance. Another, and perhaps more familiar, case is that of dolls which are made to resemble a person. These may contain fingernail clippings or hair from the person who is represented. Pins may then be driven through the image, causing, it is hoped by the magician, pain or even actual, bodily harm to the subject. This is familiar in things like the Voodoo rituals of Haiti and supposedly works because the fingernails or hair clippings retain some contact with the person to whom they belonged.

Readers are doubtless asking themselves how all this ties in with Europe's first wizards. Anybody who has grown to adulthood in the Western World is likely to have a very clear image of what the Devil looks like. He has horns growing from his head and walks on cloven hoofs. It is very odd that we should know such physical details about the leader of the forces of darkness and this chapter will be an exploration of, and quest for, what might be termed the Horned God. In Europe, successive waves of migration and invasion have superimposed various religious systems and sets of beliefs one upon the other, like a medieval palimpsest. Each leaves its mark, often in the form of superstitions or folk tales. These shape our society even now, in the up-to-date and sophisticated electronic world of the twenty-first century. Readers might, for instance, wonder why the image of a hooded man flying across the sky at about the time of the Winter Solstice, accompanied by his horned cult-animals, still haunts our childhood memories.

Antlers and horns on the heads of semi-divine beings, or upon the heads of the animals upon which they ride or which draw their chariots, are a continuing theme from the very earliest days of humans in Europe and run like a thread through a lot of folklore and legend. That children today should look from their windows at around the time of the Winter Solstice and half expect to see animals with antlers galloping across the sky is not in the least bit surprising. Indeed, an interest in and references to antlers and horned animals might even pre-date our own human race, that is to say the species *Homo sapiens*. Ancient burials of humans who were laid to rest with antlers and bones from deer or other horned animals are known from as far back as 100,000 years ago. A cave in Israel at a place called Qafzeh contains the grave of a child buried with deer antlers laid on his breast. Other children's bodies had deers' horns placed in their hands before their graves were filled in. At Amud, also in Israel, a Neanderthal child was buried with a bone from a deer. At another Israeli site called Kebara, a Neanderthal child was interred with the horn of a rhinoceros.

For some reason animals with horns or tusks, especially deer, but sometimes rhinoceros, goats, wild boar, mammoths and cattle, have from the earliest times been seen as special and bones from such animals are often found in the graves of prehistoric people – even the Neanderthals, who preceded us as the dominant human species. Antlers and horns are a recurring theme throughout the cultures of Europe and the Middle East. From the Neanderthals in Israel 100,000 years ago to the hunter-gatherers of Scandinavia 80,000 years later and even down to historical times, the practice of including the antlers, teeth and bones of deer in graves has been carried on since the very first *Homo sapiens* left their ancestral homeland in Africa.

There seems to be something about animals with horns, antlers or tusks which for tens of thousands of years held an almost hypnotic fascination for humanity. It has been speculated that this is because such animals were the largest and most powerful which early men and women encountered and were held in reverence and awe for that reason. They also provided the bulk of food, especially in winter. The largest and most majestic beast in Britain today is the deer, the male of which has of course antlers. The next largest and most powerful animal is the wild boar, which has tusks. If we look back to the Britain of 50,000 years ago, the biggest animals also had horns and tusks. The mightiest animal of all in Europe was the mammoth, which was essentially an elephant covered with fur. Like the more familiar elephant of today, the mammoth had tusks. There was also the woolly rhinoceros, which had a horn on the tip of its nose. As we noted above, a Neanderthal child was buried with the horn of such an animal.

Prehistoric people had an intimate relationship with these horned, antlered and tusked animals. They hunted them not only for their meat, but also the antlers and tusks which they bore. Even without carving or otherwise altering them, deers' antlers made very useful tools. In the English county of Norfolk are flint mines, known locally as Grimes' Graves. To obtain the flints, a lot of chalk had to be first removed and for this, deer antlers were used as pickaxes. Most of the excavations of the monuments which made up the ritual landscape of Britain, the causewayed enclosures and so on, were dug out by using antlers as picks and shovels. The antlers could also be fashioned into all sorts of useful things such as needles and fish hooks. The skin of the deer could be turned into clothing and the bones too used as a raw material. To see how Europeans once viewed the deer, one only has to look at the way in which the Lapps of northern Scandinavia use every part of the reindeer with which they travel.

The Lapps, more correctly known as Sami, herd reindeer across the northernmost parts of Europe. Reindeer need no fodder, being capable of living where few other animals are able to flourish, scraping lichen and moss from bare rocks for their sustenance. The Lapps drink the milk of reindeer, use their dried dung for campfires, turn their antlers into everything from buttons to cups and spoons, eat their flesh and turn the hides into tents and clothes. In return, they protect the herd from wolves and other predators. This is a symbiotic relationship, from which both reindeer and men benefit.

The close association which the modern-day Sami or Lapps have with the horned creatures with whom they are associated has built up over the course of thousands of years. The dealings which prehistoric men and women had with animals bearing antlers, horns or tusks was of course bloodier and more adversarial. Men and beasts came together in the hunt. The hunt and the ceremonies and practices associated with it tie in very closely with our quest for the earliest origins of wizards and their magic.

It is obvious that hunting mammoths, wild boar, bison, wild oxen and even stags can be a tricky and dangerous enterprise, which is why any sort of supernatural aid would be welcomed. This is where wizardry and magic came in, because this could give one a definite edge when facing up to an enraged mammoth. Specifically, sympathetic magic was brought into play. We may be fairly sure that this is the case because of a number of converging pieces of evidence from the distant past.

Illustration 9 shows a drawing which may be familiar to readers. It is of the so-called 'Sorcerer of Trois-Frères'. Just before the First World War, a cave was discovered in southern France which was named the 'Sanctuary' by those who first explored it. The grotto, dating back around 13,000 years, was clearly a shrine or temple of some kind. The walls were covered in drawings and paintings of animals and there was also a stunningly realistic sculpture of two bison – more horned animals. On one wall of the cave was sketched an enigmatic figure. This had both human and animal characteristics. The feet were human, but the rest of the body combined features of both a man and a deer. The head was crowned with antlers. There was considerable speculation about the exact nature of this artwork. Did it show a man dressed up as a deer for some ritual involved with hunting perhaps? Or was it a creature akin to a werewolf; a man turning into a deer? Another possibility was that this was the depiction of a divine being who combined both human and animal qualities, something like the Greek god Pan. Pan, it will be recalled, had both horns and cloven hoofs. He was similar to the Hindu god Peshan and it is thought that both had their pattern from an Indo-European or Yamnaya original. He may be seen in Illustration 15.

Because horned animals were so mighty and strong and provided sustenance in the form of their meat, it was only natural that primitive people in Europe should think of enhancing a human by the addition of horns, this suggesting a man or woman with unnaturally great power or strength. The human with antlers or horns was thus a superhuman being. This figure, the person with horns, is a theme which runs through the history of Europe. It is sometimes difficult to work out if such beings are minor gods or specially enhanced men. Illustration 10 shows us a strange figure, human but with antlers. This image is from a 2,000-year-old cauldron which was recovered from a bog in Denmark. This is sometimes assumed to be the Celtic god known as Cernunnos, regarded by many as the archetypal horned god. He may be seen in Illustration 11, carved on a block of limestone. This sculpture dates from roughly the same time as the one in Illustration 10.

In 1712 a crypt was being excavated beneath the cathedral of Notre-Dame in Paris. A block of limestone was unearthed dated back 2,000 years to the time when the Romans occupied this part of France. A limestone pillar was found, which had originally been a monument set up in what was then the Roman settlement of Lutetia in the first century AD. It became known as the Pillar of the Boatmen and featured bas-reliefs of various Celtic deities, along with their names. The god shown in Illustration 11 bore the name of Cernunnos.

It is fairly obvious when looking at the image of Cernunnos from around the time of Christ that he has a human head, but with antlers sprouting from it. From these horns hang torcs, which were a symbol of royalty among the Celts who lived in Western Europe at that time. Torcs were elaborate golden rings worn about the neck to indicate status. They were, roughly speaking, analogous to crowns. The figure from the Gundestrup Cauldron also has a torc, but he is holding it up, one might almost say brandishing it, perhaps to establish his credentials as an aristocrat or perhaps even a king. In another image from the French city of Rheims, Cernunnos is show wearing a torc. The implication is most likely that the Horned God was actually the king of all the gods in the Celtic pantheon. He is not, of course, a merely Celtic god. His origins lie far further back in time than that. He is intimately associated with earlier representations of figures whose heads sport antlers or horns.

What about the idea though that the 'Sorcerer' of Trois-Frères was actually dressing up as a deer for some reason of his own? There we are on firm ground, because we know without a shadow of a doubt that dressing up as deer and putting antlers on their heads is something which men have been doing for 11,000 years or more. What's more, we have a pretty shrewd idea why they have been doing so.

In 1948 an amateur archaeologist came across some interesting finds at a place called Star Carr in the English county of Yorkshire. Realizing the importance of what he had found, he notified an expert in the field and the following year an archaeologist called Graham Clark began excavating the site, which he did between 1949 and 1951. It turned out that this had been a seasonal hunters' camp, where people returned year after year for centuries to stay for a few months at a time and hunt all kinds of animals, ranging from red deer to hedgehogs. It was the deer which were of great interest, because in addition to the discarded bones of deer which had been killed and eaten, Clark found something quite fascinating. There were twenty-one skulls of red deer which had been shaped so that they could be worn on the head. Holes had been drilled in the skulls so that leather thongs could hold them securely on the head of the person wearing this bizarre headgear, which was complete with antlers. It can hardly be doubted that anybody wearing one of these things would have looked very much like the Sorcerer of Trois-Frères. One of these may be seen in Illustration 13.

There has been some debate as to the purpose of the antler headdresses found at Star Carr. One possibility might be that they were fixed on the head and enabled a hunter to creep up on a deer unexpectedly. This is probably not as likely as that they were used by prehistoric shamans as part of magic rituals, designed to ensure success in the hunt. We know that deer antlers have been used for just this purpose in more recent times. Before looking at this, some readers may be scratching their heads and wondering what shamans actually are or were.

'Shaman' is a Siberian word and it is in Siberia that the idea of the shaman has its roots, although from there it spread in prehistoric times to North America, where it has entered the language in common usage. To go off at a slight tangent, it will be remembered that when a crowd of angry and discontented citizenry stormed the Capitol in Washington in January 2021, one figure in particular stood out from the others and became something of a *leitmotif* for the whole affair. This was a strange-looking man whose face was daubed with paint and wore on his head a furry hood with horns protruding from it. The similarity with the Sorcerer of Trois-Frères was striking. In the aftermath of the chaos, this individual was arrested and identified himself as the Q-Anon Shaman, Q-Anon being a right-wing conspiracy theory. It was fascinating to see how at a time of crisis, even in the twenty-first century, the figure of the horned shaman re-emerged as a matter of course in a new guise.

Traditionally, the shaman is in contact with both this world and that of the spirits or the dead. He can communicate with the dead, take messages to and fro between the world of living people and the spirit world. He is also able to divine the future and help people with magical spells and rituals. He is the prototype for what we in Europe call wizards and it is very likely that our concept of wizards and witches grew in part from what was faintly remembered about the shamans of Europe and Asia long before writing was devised and so history recorded. That a straight line connects the shamans of the Palaeolithic era to the modern world may be seen when we look at Illustration 12. This is a drawing which was made by a traveller in Siberia in the seventeenth century.

The shaman in this drawing is helping to bring success in the hunt for his tribe. He did this by imitating a strong, healthy animal and then mimicking the animal's suffering, injury and death. Travellers were most impressed by the death throes which were acted out. On his head, the shaman wore an antlered headdress precisely similar to those found at the hunters' camp of Star Carr.

If we compare the drawing of the Siberian shaman in Illustration 12 with that of the Sorcerer of Trois-Frères, we can see at once that there is a similarity. Looking now at the antler headpieces from Star Carr, shown in Illustration 13, it is not hard to see a common theme. What are these people doing, fixing deer's antlers on their heads in this peculiar fashion? The most likely explanation is that these form part of a ritual of sympathetic magic. This means acting something out in the hope that the actions performed will be imitated in the real word. By enacting a successful hunt we will make the actual hunt end in success. A man dons the antlers and moves about like a deer. Others mime the act of firing arrows or hurling spears at him, whereupon he makes actions symbolic of a deer's death-agony. All this must be done with the necessary incantations, which the shaman will explain to those participating in the ritual.

It seems almost beyond belief that such a magic dance should still be taking place in Europe today, but at the same time that a Dutch explorer was drawing a Siberian shaman with antlers on top of his head, the first written account was being made in Staffordshire of what must surely be part of the same tradition. Something akin to a morris dance had been taking place in the village of Abbots Bromley for many years, although it was first described in writing in 1686. Known as the 'Horn Dance', it entailed six pairs of reindeer antlers mounted on wooden posts being carried around the streets, accompanied by some of the characters from more traditional dances of this kind, a man in a dress called 'Maid Marion' and a hobby-horse. There was another dancer, a boy with a bow and arrow. His role was to fire imaginary arrows at the men brandishing the antlers. Nobody knows how long the Abbots Bromley dance has been taking place, but it looks exactly like the ritualized hunt intended to bring, by means of sympathetic magic, success in the real hunt.

For many years, cynics claimed that the Abbots Bromley dance had only been going since the Tudor period at the earliest. In 1976 though, a sliver of one of the reindeer antlers was tested by means of carbon-dating and showed that the animals to which these horns had belonged must have been alive in 1065. This means that the dance was taking place at least a thousand years ago and very possibly for much longer than that. The present sets of antlers might well be replacements for older ones.

The man with antlers or horns on his head can symbolize the hunted stag, but as a wizard, he can also stand in for the Horned God. There is a long tradition of wizards and priests doing this, standing for an absent deity. The deity in this case is an avatar or incarnation of a Yamnaya original, whom we can only try to reconstruct by examining later images. Pan is one of these and another is the Lord of the Animals, seen in a seal from the ancient city of Mohenjo-daro. This was found in 1918 and dates from over 2000 BC. It shows a horned man sitting cross-legged and surrounded by animals. The Pashupati seal, as it is known, has been thought to show an early version of one of the Hindu gods, partly because the figure is sitting in a traditional yogic position. The Lord of the Animals or Master of the Animals is a visual motif familiar in India, the Middle East and Europe. Whether he is a god or a man adopting the role of a god is not clear. On a Celtic artefact, the Gundestrup Cauldron, the Lord of the Animals is shown very clearly. He may be seen in Illustration 10.

The Lord of the Animals as seen in Illustration 10 is of a man with antlers on his head. Whether these are growing naturally from his skull or, like the Siberian shaman in Illustration 12, have been attached somehow is not clear. That this individual has mastery over animals is obvious though. Like the figure from the Pashupati seal he sits in a pose reminiscent of those used in yoga and in his left hand holds a huge snake by the throat.

Horns or antlers are traditionally associated with masculine strength. We hear an echo of such primitive beliefs to this day when we think of the 'stag parties' of unmarried young men. Horns on the human head are a symbol of virility and sometimes divinity. When the ancient Celts who once lived in Britain wished to appear fearsome or particularly masculine, they wore helmets with horns, in imitation of their deities. One such helmet, dating back some 2,000 years, may be seen in Illustration 6. It was recovered from the River Thames, into which it had almost certainly been flung as part of the sacrifices in water about which we have already learned. True, the horns are exceedingly stylized, but there cannot be the least doubt as to what they are meant to represent. Models of either warriors or gods from roughly the same period have been found, wearing similar horned helmets.

Readers are invited once more to examine and compare Illustrations 9, 10, 11 and 15. The precise purposes might be obscure, but it can hardly be doubted when looking at these images that we are seeing imperfect copies of some original, even if it is only an imaginary one. The Horned God has almost vanished now from our awareness and the only time we in the West are ever likely to call him to mind is in the degraded form of the Christian Devil. The only modern religion which still honours the Horned God is Jainism in India. There, the protector of children for Jains is known as Naigamesha. He is variously depicted as having either a goat's or stag's head.

It is time to look at the first identifiable wizard. We are certainly able to deduce the existence of shamans or wizards in the distant past, by looking at cave paintings or archaeological remains, but such people are forever likely to be shadowy and indistinct; we will never know anything about them, other than that they existed. The prototype for all subsequent wizards though, we do know. He was a man who believed, or at the least claimed, that he was channelling the spirit of a god. Perhaps he genuinely thought of himself as an avatar or incarnation of a god. We know that this man lived over 4,000 years ago. Before describing this early wizard, it might be helpful if we consider first the nature of deity.

We in the West are so used to the concept of God as a perfect being that we struggle with the idea of gods being deceitful and cruel or argumentative and unreliable. The benevolence and omnipotence of the deity is, after all, taken for granted, even among atheists! We may not believe in God, but we know what he would be like if he did exist. For almost the whole of human history though, gods have had far more in common with ordinary, fallible men and women than they have with any abstract notions of perfection. This is why gods and goddesses had no difficulty coming down to earth and passing themselves off as one of us; apart from their greater powers and immortality, they thought and behaved more or less like anybody else in the world. This could make life a little unnerving for the Indo-Europeans and their descendants, because you never knew when you were going to bump into an off-duty god!

We looked at the *Iliad* and found that it provides us with a good illustration of how the Indo-Europeans viewed their gods. It is based on oral traditions from around 1250 BC, only a matter of centuries after the arrival of Indo-European culture in Greece. The *Iliad* tells how the Trojan War was inextricably mixed up with some poor behaviour among the gods and goddesses of the time. They aided either the Greeks or Trojans, according to their own prejudices, and even came down, disguised as mortals, to involve themselves in the war for the side which they supported. Their appearance and conduct on earth was such that it was only later that those meeting them wondered if they had perhaps, unwittingly, met Apollo in person.

To give another example of this strange idea of gods visiting the earth incognito, the Roman poet Ovid tells the story of Baucis and Philemon, a poor couple who invite Zeus and Hermes into their home, under the impression that they are weary travellers. They receive their reward for this act of charity, when the two gods destroy the land for miles around because of the wickedness of those living there. Only Baucis and Philemon are spared from the general destruction. Some readers may perhaps be growing a little restless by now and wondering what all this has to do with the origins of wizards and witches, but there was a purpose to discussing these Greek and Roman fables and legends. These were not the only gods to come down to earth in this way. Our exploration now takes us to the most prosaic place imaginable; the East London district of Dagenham, formerly site of the Ford factory.

Chapter 6

The First Wizard

In 1922, Dagenham was still an Essex village which had not yet been engulfed by the sprawling suburbs of London. When sewer pipes were being laid on some marshland, where later the Ford car factory would be built, a curious piece of wood was found in one of the trenches which were being dug. It was a crude and grotesque representation of a human being, about 18in (46cm) long. The figure had legs, but no arms, and a head which was disproportionately large for the body. Between the legs was a round hole, which was probably a socket for a penis to be attached. This article, which became known as the Dagenham Idol, may be seen in Illustration 14. It was buried in the peaty marsh alongside the skeleton of a deer, which both provides a link to the idea of antlers and horns at which we looked in the last chapter and also suggests strongly that this was a deliberate sacrifice.

The Dagenham Idol is very similar to one found in a Danish bog in the late nineteenth century, known as the Broddenbjerg Idol, and they both fall into the category of what is sometimes known as 'pole gods'. They are almost certainly cult figures; representations of gods which were set up to be venerated. This was once a popular practice in northern Europe and tree-trunks with crudely carved features were set up in forest clearings, where worshippers danced around them. In Germany, they were known as irminsuls. A very famous irminsul was erected in a glade in what is now Germany, a huge tree-trunk which formed the focal point for celebrations of the Norse religion by the Saxons who lived in the area. Charlemagne, a devout Christian, had this idol hacked down in 772 AD.

Mention has been made of the tall tree-trunks, wooden posts whose remains were found near Stonehenge during the construction of a car park near the monument. These had been erected some 10,000 years ago and suggests that such pole gods are among the oldest signs of religious worship in Europe. Of course, we still have in Britain the last vestiges of the worship of pole gods, although they are never referred to as such. Rituals involving these pole gods were practised widely until only a few decades ago. We know these idols as Maypoles. The setting up of a tall wooden pole and the dancing which takes place around it is a last survival of the custom of worshipping a wooden idol. It is for this reason that the Church has often frowned upon, and sometimes forbidden, the celebration of May Day. It is perhaps no coincidence that such festivities take place at the same time as the Celtic festival of Beltane.

There are two very interesting things about both the Dagenham Idol and the Broddenbjerg Idol, which was found in Denmark, the first of which is their age. The one from Denmark was dated to 500 BC. The Dagenham Idol was carbon-dated to 2250 BC, making it one of the earliest attempts to depict a human figure in the form of a sculpture ever found in Europe. It was made in either the late Neolithic or early Bronze Age. The other interesting thing about these idols was that in both cases, the left eye was shown to be either missing or injured. In the figure from Broddenbjerg one eye is neatly carved and the other shown just by an incised line. The Dagenham Idol shows the same effect, by having a large, deep pit for the right eye and a shallow indentation for the left. In short, if these *were* meant to represent gods, then the god depicted had one eye either missing or injured.

We pause at this point and consider the concept of the one-eyed god. Of course, this does not at all tie in with our modern religious ideas, in which the deity is, by definition, perfect. One can hardly imagine an image of God the Father in a Christian church sporting an eye-patch! Do we know of any god venerated in Europe who had lost an eye? That is to say, can we think of a god who started out with two eyes, like everybody else, but then somehow came to lose one of them? There are of course monstrous giants in ancient stories such as the cyclops, one of whom Odysseus and his men fell foul of, according to Homer. These creatures though naturally had only one eye. The same applies to other legendary beings. We occasionally read accounts of human heroes who have lost an eye, but seldom a god. Let us sum up what we may reasonably assume about all this.

The Dagenham Idol and also the one from Broddenbjerg are both likely to be depictions of gods, idols set up to be venerated. They show gods in human form, men who have once had two eyes, but somehow lost one of them. They are so similar, that it seems almost certain that they belong to the same tradition. One was found in Denmark, which would later be the home of the Vikings, the place where the Norse gods were worshipped. One of those Norse gods became a man and walked the earth. He had only one eye. Given all this, it surely requires no great stretch of the imagination to conclude that the cult object uncovered in Dagenham is meant to be the god who would 3,000 years later be known as Odin. Odin, ruler of the Norse gods, was also known as Wotan and Woden. We encounter his name every week, for 'Wednesday' is none other than a corruption of 'Woden's Day'. Other days of the week named after Norse gods and goddesses are Tuesday, 'Tyr's Day', Thursday, which is 'Thor's Day' and also Friday, which is 'Freya's Day'.

One other point might be made and that is that analysis of the Dagenham Idol showed that it was made from a piece of Scots Pine, a tree far more associated with northern Europe than with the Thames Valley. This makes it likely that this is where the Dagenham Idol came from: it was imported into England thousands of years before the Romans invaded.

All of which brings us neatly to the point at which we have been aiming, which is the origin of the tradition of wizards in Europe and in particular the first who may be identified in some way, rather than just being a shaman painted on the wall of a cave. The first wizard, in fact, about whom we might be able to learn specific traditions and even facts. If that figure dug up from a peat marsh in England really did represent Odin, then it might help if we review what we know about Odin and see if it ties in with both the idea that the wooden image unearthed in Dagenham might represent this one-eyed god and also that he could be the prototype for some of our modern ideas about the appearance and lifestyle of wizards.

Odin was chief in the pantheon of Norse gods and goddesses, about whom many of us learned at school. Because northern Germany and Scandinavia, where these particular deities were venerated, was a part of Europe which was outside the Roman Empire, old ideas and traditions lingered on there for a lot longer than they did elsewhere. Just as in places like Lithuania the earliest form of the Indo-European was preserved, because it was a backwater, so too did older ideas about sorcery and religion linger on in Scandinavia and northern Germany, long after the rest of the continent had been successively Romanized and then fallen under the sway of Christianity. The Dagenham Idol pre-dates not only Christianity, but even Judaism. At the time it was carved, Abraham had not yet set off from Ur in the Chaldees.

Because those living to the north of the Roman Empire retained their own cultural traditions, without getting muddled up with the Roman gods or Christianity, it is likely that what we know of the Norse religion gives us an insight into a much earlier view of Indo-European religious traditions than any other. Thor the thunder god, Odin the ruler of the gods and Frigg the goddess of fertility and abundance, are perhaps the earliest archetypes whom we have for these deities in Europe; predating either the Greek or Roman ideas and images.

According to both the Prose *Edda* and the Poetic *Edda*, Icelandic sagas from which we gain most of the information which we have about the supposed natures of the Norse gods, Odin was renowned for his magical ability; in other words, he was seen as a sorcerer. He was the oldest of the gods and also the wisest. He had not always been wise though; he had to seek wisdom. This seems very strange to people today, most of whom have been raised to think of God as being all-knowing and all-powerful. When he decided that he wished to become the wisest of the gods, Odin went to visit a minor god of whom few people will have heard. This was Mimir, who was the guardian of a magic well called Mimmisbrunnr, which simply means Mimir's well. Those who drank from this well acquired wisdom. The guardian of the well would not allow just anybody to take a draught from his well though; he always exacted a price, even from the chief god. In his case, Mimir demanded that Odin sacrifice one of his eyes and cast it into the well. This, Odin did and was rewarded with a horn full of water from the well, which was how he became wiser than any man or god.

We looked earlier at the tradition which is still extant in Europe, of casting money into fountains and wells, which is of course where the idea of the 'wishing well' arises. Mimmisbrunnr may be seen as the archetypal wishing well. Odin wished to acquire wisdom and was expected in return to deposit something of value. In his case though, so momentous was the wish that he was required to leave a gift of vastly more value than a little loose change. The principle though, of Odin's sacrifice and our casting of coins into a wishing well in the local park is precisely similar.

Not only did he sacrifice one of his eyes in pursuit of wisdom, Odin gave his very life. According to Norse cosmology, a huge tree called the Yggdrasil or World-tree passes through the various parts of the world. Upon this mysterious tree Odin hung for nine days and nights, pierced by a spear, until he died. He was brought back to life by magic and when he was resurrected, he understood all manner of wonders which were hidden from the other gods. One of these was the secret of the runes, the angular letters used by the Norsemen to make inscriptions on wood, stone and bone. Odin also, as a consequence of all that he endured, became a seer; somebody who could foretell the future.

The Icelandic *Eddas* give us a good description of Odin's appearance and also some idea of how he conducted himself. His practice of visiting our world in the guise of an old man is mentioned and he is described as having the appearance of an old man with a grey beard, carrying a staff and with a floppy hat which makes it difficult sometimes to see his face. He wore this so that he would not be identified by the fact that he was missing an eye. He also wears a grey or blue cloak. This is of course Gandalf, even down to his hat. Readers of *The Lord of the Rings* will know that Gandalf was not really a man at all, but one of the Maior, angelic messengers from the realm of the gods. In this respect too, he resembles Odin, in that he is only disguised as a mortal.

That Odin was the pattern for Tolkien's Gandalf is not seriously in doubt; Tolkien himself admitted as much. Odin though has had an even greater influence on our culture than just appearing as a character in a fantasy novel. One of Odin's many titles in the *Edda* is Yule Father and he is associated with feasting and revels at midwinter. Although it has a slightly archaic sound to it, the word 'Yule' is still current in modern English, as in 'Yuletide greetings'. Instead of the floppy hat he sometimes wore when visiting earth, Odin was also known to cover his head with a hood as well. Thus we have arriving in the middle of December an old man with a long white beard, whose face is partly concealed by a hood and who goes by the name of Yule Father or Father Yule. Nor are these the only similarities with the Father Christmas for whom children anxiously wait on Christmas Eve.

In Scandinavia and Germany, before the countries there became fully Christianised, children expected Odin, as Yule Father, to visit their homes around Midwinter's Day, the Winter Solstice on 21 December. They would fill their shoes with straw and carrots, leaving them by the hearth. Odin rode an eight-legged horse called Sleipnir and this was supposed to provide fodder for Odin's mount if he should come in the night. In the morning, the straw and carrots were gone and the shoes filled with sweets.

Here then is a custom which must surely have persisted in folk memory, that is to say passed down orally through the generations for at least a thousand years and almost certainly much longer. Although it is less common today, some children in Europe still place a glass of an alcoholic beverage and a few carrots out on Christmas Eve for Father Christmas and his reindeer. The wizard or demigod in a chariot being drawn by horned animals did not begin with Father Christmas. We have seen the startling resemblance which Odin Allfather bears to Father Christmas, but another Norse god had a curious mode of transport which we might recognize.

In the saga known as the Prose *Edda* it is related that Thor drives a chariot pulled by two goats, called Tanngnjóstr and Tanngrisnir. These names mean teeth-barer and teeth-grinder. The similarity between Father Christmas and his reindeer is striking. It is likely that both legends have a common source in Indo-European mythology. This is especially so when we recollect that Father Christmas, in older stories told as late as the early nineteenth century, rode not in a sleigh pulled by reindeer but rather one drawn by a goat. In some old illustrations he is actually shown riding a goat much as one would a horse. Illustration 17 shows such a scene.

The goat which Father Christmas rides is known in Scandinavian countries as the Yule Goat and its origins lie in the distant past, probably in a pre-Christian tradition. Over and over again, we come up against the same images and themes of the horned animals and the man of magic with an intimate connection to horned animals. Father Christmas, or the Yule Father as we might just as easily think of him, did not visit European children by himself at Christmas. He was, or so legend tells us, accompanied by a fearsome being known as Krampus.

Krampus, who is shown in Illustration 18, is of course all but identical to the Devil as portrayed in Christian mythology. The humanoid body, combined with animal features such as thick hair and a tail, and in particular the horns on his head, all tell us that this is a figure of evil. We must remark too that Krampus bears a striking resemblance to both the Lord of the Animals and the Sorcerer of Trois-Frères. In later years, Krampus was played down and modified, until he was replaced by the goat which Father Christmas is seen riding in Illustration 17, but at one time he was seen as being a natural counterpart to the benign

Father Christmas or Father Yule. Father Christmas brought presents for good boys and girls, which he carried in his sack. Krampus, on the other hand, also had a sack. His sack though was for taking things away from the houses which he visited; that is to say that he stuffed naughty children in his sack and carried them off, to be eaten according to some and drowned by other accounts.

What have we learned about Odin? In some version or another, he has been known in Europe for at least 4,000 years. At least, that is how long we know for sure that a one-eyed god from northern Europe has been around. We know too that he was not always a wise and powerful god but, like a human, had to make sacrifices to attain wisdom. Odin was also unusual among the other Norse gods, because he was a master of magic. Thor might wield tremendous power and Tyr was a mighty warrior, but they were neither of them sorcerers or wizards. That is one of the distinguishing features of Odin Allfather. We know too that he is a master of disguise and that he walks the earth looking like anybody else. Then too, he is associated with horns. Sometimes he rides a goat, at other times he is seen in a chariot or sleigh which is drawn by stags or reindeer. In the oldest legends, the Yule Father is accompanied by a half-human creature with horns on his head. The oldest image of Odin, the one-eyed god, was buried 4,000 years ago with the sacrificial offer of a stag.

Assuming that we are correct both about the identification of Odin with the one-eyed images dating back thousands of years, found both in Britain and northern Europe, and also that he was first and foremost a worker of magic and a seer, what might we reasonably hypothesize about him?

The first thing which strikes us is that his story seems human, rather than divine. Why should the king of the gods have to give an eye to take a draft from some well? Could he not do as he wished? Secondly, of course, we know that in later stories Odin is portrayed as a shape-shifter. He can adopt the form of whatever animal or person he wishes and so move around the earth in such a way that nobody is aware the chief god is among them. And yet curiously enough, as a man, he always has that missing eye. This is seemingly something of a nuisance to him, as he has to wear a hat with a floppy brim or pull a hood over his head to prevent people from spotting that giveaway clue to his true identity. There is something inconsistent and odd about this, because if he really is capable of assuming any form he wishes, why not just appear as a man with two eyes like everybody else?

The more one studies the character of Odin, as revealed in the Icelandic *Eddas*, the most extensive body of legends about him, the more Odin comes across as a real man and not a god at all. True, he has many strange powers, but most of these are the standard attributes of shamans or wizards. He can be, according to his mood, benevolent and wise or angry and irrational. He spends more time wandering around the world like Gandalf than he does sitting on a throne in Valhalla. In short, Odin appears to be part-shaman and part-god. This of course would tie in perfectly with some of the ideas at which we have already looked, that shamans sometimes channelled the spirits of the animals which were to be hunted by their tribe and at others became the very incarnation of the horned god. There is another possibility, however.

There is in Indo-European tradition a very strong idea that men and women can, under certain circumstances, be elevated to the status of immortal spirits or gods. We see a lot of this in Greek mythology. The process is known as apotheosis. Ariadne was a Cretan princess who became a goddess, Dionysus was once a man and there are many other examples. The Romans too had a similar belief and extended the idea to the extent that some emperors were deified upon their death and it became the practice to worship them in specially constructed temples. Claudius, the emperor who was responsible for invading and occupying Britain, was deified immediately upon his death and a temple devoted to his worship in the town of Colchester was one factor in precipitating the revolt led by Boudicca. We encounter a relic of this practice every year, when the summer comes round. Some of the months of the year are of course named after Roman gods. January is named after Janus, for instance. August is also named after a god, although one who was born a man. The same is true of July.

Julius Caesar was declared a living god in his own lifetime, being theoretically descended from gods. After his death, or martyrdom, Julius Caesar was raised to the status of a full god and sacrifices were made to him. Our month of July is named after this human-born divinity. Three men fought for the ultimate control of the Roman world after Caesar's assassination. These three contenders were Mark Antony, Marcus Lepidus and Caesar's nephew Octavian. Octavian emerged victorious and ended up being known as Augustus. Following his death, he too was deified and, like his uncle, had a month named after him, which is of course August.

That this religious belief was so widespread in Europe suggests that it had its origins, as with so many other aspects of European culture, in the Yamnaya belief system. Looked at from this perspective, a very plausible scenario may be constructed which explains the origin of Odin and how the one-eyed god came to be venerated thousands of years before we ever hear of the Norse god. It gives us as well some information about the very first wizard in Europe, even down to the way that he dressed.

Gods are unlikely to become physically maimed, but humans do fall prey to this misfortune. What if there was, at least 4,000 years ago, a famous shaman who was associated with the hunting of horned beasts? We know that such men existed, because of the archaeological evidence at which we have looked. This man was a mighty magician who had the reputation of somebody capable of such feats as predicting the day on which the days would begin to grow shorter or to lengthen. Again, we know that such wise men were around thousands of years ago because we see the alignment of megaliths and tombs with various equinoxes or solstices. This man was remarkable for his knowledge of the heavens and also the way in which the movements of the sun, moon and stars affected the growing of crops or the tides of the oceans. So far, we have not needed to do anything other than speculate about what is already known. What if this famous wizard was notable though for missing an eye?

It is not hard to imagine that as he wandered from tribe to tribe, stories and legends might grow up around this, the most renowned shaman of the late Neolithic or early Bronze Age. It would be only human nature for the one-eyed wizard to encourage fantastic tales about his powers and perhaps even his origins. What would be more likely than that he would turn the loss of an eye to his advantage and use it to enhance the awe in which he was already held? Perhaps he might claim to have traded one of his eyes with a supernatural entity, so that he would gain knowledge which he was now using to the benefit of the scattered communities which the Yamnaya had established in Europe. As a wandering worker of magic, far from his home, it is unlikely that anybody would be able to contradict any stories which he told about his birth or previous life.

The tales told over the years about the strange old man with only one eye, who was able to turn up at a village and tell them how many days until they should plant their seeds or even perhaps when the next eclipse of the moon would occur must have been an astonishingly powerful memory and it would be quite understandable if the stories and anecdotes turned over the years into myth. Did odd details about his clothing and general appearance get handed down from one generation to the next? Perhaps this wizard really did wear a hood or floppy hat at one time, because he was self-conscious about the missing eye. It is also conceivable that he wore a cloak and carried a walking staff.

It does not take long for legends involving the supernatural to spring up and take hold, even in the relatively modern world. One only has to think about the story of the Angels of Mons during the First World War to see how this happens. In 1914, following the British army's first military engagement in 1914, author Arthur Machen wrote a short story for the London newspaper *The Evening News*. It was called 'The Bowmen' and imagined one of the hard-pressed British soldiers appealing to St George and his unit then being aided by phantom archers, the spirits of English soldiers from the Battle of Agincourt, nearly 500 years before.

It did not take long for the rumour to spread that the story of the spectral bowmen was actually a true one. The following year a spiritualist magazine wrote that an angel had defended the British army at the Battle of Mons in 1914 and from then on it was accepted as fact by many people that supernatural entities had aided the army. This was in the world of telephones, aeroplanes, radio, cinema and internal combustion engines. If such a ridiculous legend could spring up in the modern world, how much easier would this have been in the pre-literate society of Europe 4,000 or 5,000 years earlier?

It has been said that God is no more than Man writ large and there can be little doubt that primitive societies do tend to create gods in their own image. The figure of Odin has such human attributes that is quite likely that he was modelled originally on a real person. He may well be in fact the first identifiable wizard of whom we have any knowledge.

Chapter 7

The Wild Hunt

In the last chapter we saw how a human wizard might have been elevated to the status of a god. It is time now to look at how this deified figure might have found himself portrayed in various other guises, sometimes as a legendary hero and at other in a supernatural or diabolical form.

Once agriculture had become established in Europe, the most important aid which any wizard could render to a community would be advice on when they should plant seeds and harvest crops. Before that time though, the crucial task of the earliest shamans was almost certainly to provide magical help in the hunt, upon which the health, prosperity and very survival of a tribe or clan might depend. This was done sometimes by imitating the object of the hunt, normally a creature with antlers, horns or tusks, and on other occasions pretending to be the successful hunter slaying the beast. The shaman identified so fully with both hunter and hunted that his identity became confused. At other times, the shaman or wizard stood in for the god, becoming the personification or incarnation of the horned Lord of the Animals.

These are difficult and unfamiliar concepts for many people in the modern world. Perhaps a parallel maybe drawn with priests in the Catholic Church. When Catholics go to confession, their sins are forgiven, ostensibly by the priest. But the priest is not really speaking as a human. He is taking on the character of the god whom he serves and it is thus that he acquires the power to forgive sin. In the same way, when he magically changes the communion wafer and wine into the flesh and blood of the god, he does so because he is channelling the divine power. This is just what happened when the Stone Age shaman donned his antlers and animal skin and took part in a magical ceremony. Sometimes he became the hunted beast but at other times he was the Horned God himself. This was wizardry indeed and it can be little wonder that one of these shamans came to be recognized as the first true wizard.

Hunting was a vital activity during the times when the Neanderthals occupied Europe and also for many thousands of years after they had been replaced by our own ancestors, the *Homo sapiens* who are modern humanity. Protein was essential if a tribe was to remain healthy and their children grow to adulthood. The source of that protein was animals, which of course had to be hunted and killed.

There are two basic types of hunt. On the one hand, there is the earliest kind, which may be called ambush hunting. This how Neanderthals and the first modern humans most likely sought their prey. They found a place where the animals came, perhaps in search of water, and then concealed themselves near this spot. It required a good deal of patience, but little complicated planning. Sooner or later a deer might come down to a stream to drink and then the hunters would leap out and hurl their spears. We still see ambush hunting in Europe and America. Every time an angler sits quietly on the bank of a river and waits for a fish to take his bait, then he is playing the part of the ambush hunter. By and large, ambush hunting is free of great hazard. There is of course the chance that a stag might catch somebody with an antler, but generally it was a fairly quiet affair. The animals would appear, the spears were thrown and those animals which were not wounded or killed would flee in fear.

The other main type of hunting is by pursuit. The British custom of fox hunting is an instance of this. Men and hounds chase an animal, hoping to exhaust it until it can be overtaken and killed. Hunting animals in this way, especially if they are large and dangerous, requires fluent use of language and instant understanding of orders and changes of plan. When hunting a mammoth or bison, there would be little time for waiting until a member of the hunt could work out what was required of him. It was a fast-moving operation and demanded quicker wits than simply hiding behind bushes and then slinging a spear at something. This kind of hunting is really like close-quarters combat. In an ambush, the animals are able to flee and their flight is unimpeded. When you are chasing them, they may very well turn and fight. If your putative prey is large and dangerous, say wild boar, bison or a mammoth, members of the hunting party can easily find themselves changing from hunter to prey, if they are cornered by an angry beast with horns. This reminds us of the rituals of which we have talked, where the shaman changes roles seamlessly between hunter and prey and then back again.

These ideas about the sort of rituals engaged in before the hunt are more than just educated guesswork. Illustration 12 shows a seventeenth-century shaman in Siberia, who conducted just these very magical rites to ensure success in the hunt. He is even wearing antlers and bears an uncanny resemblance to the Sorcerer of Trois-Frères.

When some activity is necessary simply to remain alive, into which category hunting most definitely fell in the prehistoric world, it is inevitable that superstitions and myths should grow up around it. Soldiers in wartime generate and perpetuate such customs as not lighting three cigarettes from the same match, lest this provided an enemy sniper with sufficient time to take careful aim. Many men on active service take to prayer and appeal to the Almighty to preserve them from harm; hence the old saying that there are no atheists in foxholes. In the case of hunting, the stories of the shamans and wizards and their changing roles as hunters and quarry, man and god, turned into an enduring and overarching myth, that of the Wild Hunt.

In antiquity, the dividing line between the man hunting a stag and the stag itself was sometimes believed to be vanishingly thin. It took only the slightest intervention from some minor deity or even a wizard's spell and roles could easily be reversed. Consider the myth of Actaeon, grandson of King Cadmus of Thebes. The young man was out hunting one day, he and his pack of hounds in hot pursuit of a stag, when he chanced upon the goddess Artemis, or Diana as she was known to the Romans, bathing in a secluded pool. Entranced by the sight, Actaeon dismounted and crept closer. He had never seen such a beautiful sight as the goddess, standing naked by the side of the pool. When she and her attendant nymphs became aware of him, Artemis splashed water in his face, which had the effect of transforming him from hunter to deer. Illustration 19 shows Actaeon in the moment of transformation. He is the very image of the Sorcerer of Trois-Frères, with the body of a man crowned by an antlered head. As he fled in terror, his own hounds picked up the scent and chased after him. When they caught up with him, the dogs tore Actaeon to pieces. We see in this little story the perfect interchangeability of hunter and prey.

It is time to look at another huntsman who has antlers sprouting from his head. He is a leader of the Wild Hunt. In Shakespeare's *The Merry Wives of Windsor* reference is made to a local legend. This is what is said,

> There is an old tale goes, that Herne the Hunter (sometime a keeper here in Windsor Forest) Doth all the winter-time, at still midnight Walk round about an oak, with great ragg'd horns; And there he blasts the tree, and takes the cattle, And makes milch-kine yield blood, and shakes a chain In a most hideous and dreadful manner. You have heard of such a spirit, and well you know The superstitious idle-headed eld Receiv'd, and did deliver to our age This tale of Herne the Hunter for a truth.

Who is this Herne the Hunter, with his 'great ragg'd horns'? This is an interesting point. There are a number of theories about the origin of this mysterious figure, who must have looked very much like the Sorcerer of Trois-Frères, the Siberian shaman in Illustration 12, the Lord of the Animals from the Gundestrup Cauldron and also Actaeon. One story is that he was a huntsman and gamekeeper in the forest at Windsor who one day saved a king from a deadly attack by a stag. Herne was himself mortally wounded in saving the king and a passing wizard saved his life by taking the antlers of the stag which Herne had just killed and binding them on the huntsman's head, where they began to grow quite naturally.

Anthropologist Margaret Murray, a specialist in European witchcraft, had a quite different explanation for the story of Herne. She believed him to be a British version of Cernunnos, the horned god of the Celts. It is true that there may be a linguistic connection between Cernunnos and Herne. The name Cernunnos is derived from the Latin word for 'horn' and some people believed that Herne might be a mispronunciation of 'horn'. This is fairly slender evidence though. What is certain is that the man with the antlers of a deer who haunted Windsor is an ancient figure and that he features in one of the primeval stories of Europe, the Wild Hunt.

It was the Brothers Grimm who first set out the story of the Wild Hunt as they were able to piece it together from myths and legends from all over Europe. The Wild Hunt is a troop of spectral riders and hounds which charge through the night sky at certain times of year and specific climatic conditions. It is led by various famous gods and men, depending upon which country or even district one looks at. In Germany and Scandinavia Odin or Wotan is usually said to be the master of the Wild Hunt, while in Britain there are half a dozen different versions of the legend, all with different leaders, some of whom are historical figures, but in other parts of the country the Devil himself. In Cornwall, the Wild Hunt is known as the Devil's Dandy Dogs, in the north as Gabriel's Hounds and also as the Wish-hounds. Among those said to lead the hunt in England have been Herod, Cain and of course Herne.

So what actually *is* the Wild Hunt? It is a spectral troop who gallop across the sky when thunder is rolling or the Winter Solstice is at hand. They are hunting not animals, but human souls and it can be a very dangerous sight to witness. Herne, with his antlered head, is said to

Above left: 1. A modern version of the wizard's hat, with which we are all familiar.

Above right: 2. A golden hat, dating back 3,000 years, bearing astronomical symbols.

Right: 3. The so-called 'Witch of Subeshi' wearing a hat made over 2,000 years ago. (*Jeffrey Newbury*)

4. Witches as shown in an old woodcut, wearing the immediately recognisable black, pointed hats.

Left: 5. The sword Excalibur is hurled into the lake.

Below: 6. A horned helmet recovered from the River Thames in London. (*Ealdgyth*)

Right: 7. Rumpelstiltskin, delighted at the prospect of acquiring a human baby.

Below: 8. Medieval stone coffin in London's Southwark Cathedral, with tribute of coins.

Left: 9. The 'Sorcerer of Trois Frères', a prehistoric shaman.

Below: 10. The Lord of the Animals as depicted on the Gundestrup Cauldron.

Right: 11. Cernunnos, the horned god as shown on a 2,000-year-old carving.

Below: 12. A seventeenth-century Siberian shaman enacts rituals to aid in the hunting of horned animals.

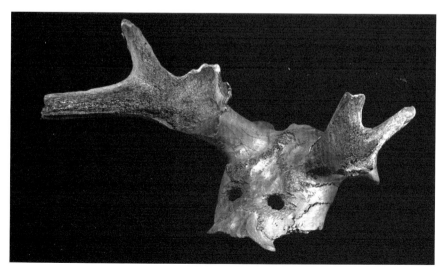

13. Deer skull used as a head-dress in Britain, 10,000 years ago.

Above left: 14. The Dagenham Idol. (*Ethan Doyle White*)

Above right: 15. The god Pan; a later avatar of Cernunnos.

Below: 16. One of the so-called 'bog bodies', sacrificial victims from the Iron Age.

Right: 17. An ancient god rides upon his cult animal.

Below: 18. The horned god visits a nineteenth-century home to punish sinful children.

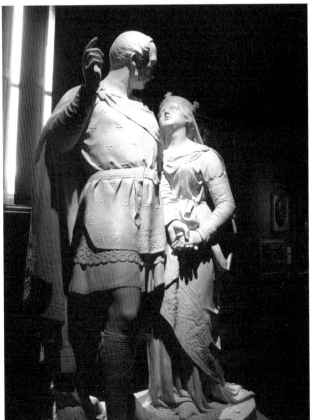

Above: 19. A human acquires antlers and changes from hunter to quarry.

Left: 20. Statue of Queen Victoria and Prince Albert dressed as medieval monarchs.

lead the hounds in Berkshire and woe betide any who do not clear the way for his horses and men. What we are really seeing in the Wild Hunt is neither a supernatural event, nor a mere fairy tale. Instead, we are being reminded of the age when hunting was not the preserve of wealthy people for amusement and sport, but rather an activity in which everybody joined, at enormous risk. The Wild Hunt is pursuit hunting and we remember that those taking part were in hazard of losing their lives at any moment as they raced at full pelt across forest and plain, chasing and attempting to bring down large animals.

This explains why the Wild Hunt is a soul-gathering exercise, because those who took part in the frenzied melee which ensued when hunted animals were run down were at constant hazard of losing their souls; being killed, in other words.

That both Odin, the archetypal wizard, and also Herne, an incarnation of the Lord of the Animals, should be said to lead the Wild Hunt is easy enough to understand. Finding the original shaman and the oldest god of Europe mixed up in a garbled remembrance of the days when hunting was so vital to human survival should come as little or no surprise. It is Herne though who is of most interest in this context. Why should we see the horned shaman or wizard accompanying the hunt? When men go into battle and fear that they might lose their very lives, religious belief can be a great comfort to them. If they are able to persuade themselves that they will be plucked from the battlefield at the moment of death and transported to paradise, they may be less apt to skulk in the background, trying to save their skins. So it was with the Wild Hunt. Before the hunt, the horned shaman would provide magical aid and he also promised the help of the Horned God during the action. This is why Herne, as an avatar of Cernunnos, is leader of the Wild Hunt in parts of England. It is too why the ancient god, the prototype of Odin, leads the cavalcade in Nordic countries.

We have followed several iterations of the Horned God, from the Sorcerer of Trois-Frères and the Lord of the Animals on the seal from Mohenjo-daro, through to Cernunnos and the god on the Gundestrup

Cauldron. The names may change, but the image remains the same. When we hear that the Cornish Dandy Dogs are led in the Wild Hunt by the Devil himself, this fits in perfectly with what we have already seen. What did the Devil look like? Why, he had horns on his head of course. With the arrival of Christianity to Europe, the old gods were demoted and reduced to the status of demons and so instead of being venerated and respected, the deposed Horned God is now feared as a devil.

In some of the more remote parts of Britain and Ireland, the memory of the Wild Hunt still lingers on. The original stories are all but forgotten now and all that remains is the fact that on thundery winter's nights old people might mutter that the Dandy Dogs are out or that the Gabriel Hounds can be heard. In this we can see the last traces of a far earlier culture, one which sought supernatural explanations for events in the natural world. The memories of such beliefs, which were circulating by mouth long before anybody devised a method of setting down a record of them permanently, are echoes of the past world. We call such oral traditions 'folk memories'.

It is possible that some readers may feel that all this talk about Horned Gods and Wild Hunts has led us down a byway which has little to do with the matter of wizards and witches. It is not so, all this background information is necessary to see in context the stories of sorcerers and shamans from which our ideas of wizards have grown. We shall in the next chapter see how such people fitted into the society in which they moved.

Chapter 8

The Place of Wizards in Society

We considered in the Introduction the landscape of some fictional or mythic realms which are based on old folklore and legend. Wagner and Tolkien, C.S. Lewis and Terry Pratchett, together with modern works in various media such as cinema films and computer games, were briefly examined. Each was loosely structured along the same tripartite society as those which we have studied. Indeed, it is hard to envision a successful fantasy story of this kind without those three ingredients, which is to say wizards, warriors and peasants. Of course, there is one slight difference, in that priests and magicians are blurred a little and combined in one function. The farmers and ordinary workers are of course present, as are the warriors.

In early societies, the role of the priest was not limited to conducting religious services. Often, he or she would undertake to foretell the future, carry out sacrifices, judge the innocence or guilt of those accused of serious crimes or summon up supernatural forces to aid their people when they were menaced by anything from a drought to an approaching enemy army. Much of the priests' work entailed what we would now regard as exercising magical powers to influence the world around them. In short, there was no clear-cut division in the ancient world between those who helped their compatriots worship the gods and those who called up supernatural forces. The roles of wizard and priest were so closely melded together that it was impossible to tell where one ended and the other began. Of course, we have echoes of this today, in a weaker form, when a Catholic priest chants an incantation or spell and turns a piece of unleavened bread into the body of the god whom he serves. It is hard to view this practice as anything other than magical. Christian priests will also attempt to invoke the help of their threefold god when war threatens, another obvious throwback to the role of wizard. Even today the British and American armies have chaplains, whose role is to try and aid the victory of their own forces over those of any enemy.

These three divisions of earthly society were mirrored in the lives of the gods. In Norse mythology, Odin represented the priest or magician, and sometimes king, Thor was the god of warriors and Freya the deity who was concerned with bringing forth food from the land. The Greek, Roman and Hindu pantheons had a similar division of labour among the gods. It was, to use the words of the Lord's Prayer, very much a case of, 'on Earth, as it is in Heaven'. In all the areas where the Indo-Europeans spread and to which they carried their language, we see the same division of labour in the religious systems which evolved. Some gods are associated with magical power, others with warfare and a third class with fertility and growth.

The power of wizards lay in their knowledge. It was this which distinguished them from warriors and farmers. These people worked with their hands, wielding sickles or swords, but it was the wizards who advised them on when and where to do so. The farmer needed to be told when to sow seed, for instance, and the wizards could also administer basic medicines, derived from berries, roots, herbs and bark. The warrior needed a good strong sword and the farmer needed a plough. Both of these useful articles were fashioned by smiths. There were rituals to be observed in the forging of a blade, whether for agriculture or war, and it was to the wizard that men looked to provide this special knowledge. Smiths were often thought to be magicians themselves in a small way, which is why some of the earliest fairy stories, dating back to the Iron Age, are about them.

The learning and wisdom of wizards was not preserved in written records. The first wizards lived in pre-literate societies and so their arcane knowledge was learned by heart and preserved orally. Very likely, it was chanted in the form of poetry, as this makes memorizing by heart much easier. This was similar to the traditions of the bard; a class of professional poets, part of whose job was to compose poetry which would allow a tribe to remember where they came from and the genealogies of the ruling dynasty and other such things. This is how the scripture of both the Hebrews and the Hindus was passed on for many centuries, before finally being written down. Unfortunately, the history of the Celts, who were the keepers of much of the lore of the Indo-Europeans, was largely obliterated before it was able to be written down. In Britain, the great sanctuary of the druids was on the Isle of Anglesey, of the coast of Wales. This was destroyed by the Roman army at about the same time that Boudicca was wreaking havoc in Colchester, London and St Albans.

We have seen the great importance of the number three to the Indo-Europeans and it is time to look at a one final example of this, which is especially concerned with wizards. This relates to the practice of capital punishment or human sacrifice among the Celts in Gaul and the Germanic tribes in northern Europe. It will probably come as no surprise by now to learn that there were, for the Celts, three chief gods. These were Esus, Taranis and Teutates. Sacrifices to each of these gods had to be performed in a certain way – by hanging, drowning and burning respectively. In the north, the three methods of capital punishment were hanging, stabbing and drowning. These three techniques for disposing of human beings were related both to the three ruling deities and also reflected the tripartite division of society. Execution or sacrifice by drowning was made to the fertility god or goddess, that by stabbing or burning to the god of warriors and hanging indicated a death offered to the chief god. It will of course be remembered that Odin, the chief god of the Norse mythology, was both the archetype for wizards such as Tolkien's Gandalf and that he also was hanged on the Ash-Yggdrasil tree. One of his titles alludes to this; he was sometimes referred to as the Lord of the Gallows.

In some forms of human sacrifice in antiquity, all three methods of execution would be employed on one victim, a practice which has become known as the threefold death. In 1984 the naked body of a man was recovered from a bog in the English county of Cheshire. Peat cutting had been taking place and it was this which brought the corpse to light. At first, there was a suspicion that the body might be that of a modern murder victim, but examination revealed that it had been concealed in the peat for something like 2,000 years. The cold and acidic water of the peat bog had kept the corpse in a remarkably complete state; the skin, hair internal organs and even the fingernails were all present. Lindow Man, as he became known due to the location where the preserved corpse was unearthed, had met a singularly gruesome and unpleasant death. Forensic analysis suggested that he had been strangled with a ligature, struck on the head hard enough to shatter the bone, had his throat cut and then been placed face down in the water of the bog.

Lindow Man was not the first such corpse to be found. Other 'bog bodies' had been found in Denmark, Germany, Ireland and other countries. Many had met violent ends and died from more than one cause. Typically, there were fractured skulls, twisted nooses around the neck, cut throats and other injuries. Victims of this kind all seemed to have met their deaths in the Iron Age. The fact that they had been attacked in two or three distinct ways, combined with the lack of clothing, suggested that these were not ordinary murder victims, people perhaps waylaid, assaulted, robbed and then thrown in the nearest pool. All the indications were that the deaths had a ritual aspect to them, as part of either a religious sacrifice or judicial execution. It was the nature of the wounds, together with the means of disposing of the corpses, which caused archaeologists to plump for the first of these hypotheses. One of these victims, found in Denmark, may be seen in Illustration 16.

That naked bodies from Iron Age Europe had ligatures or nooses around their necks, as did Lindow Man, could not help but suggest hanging and an association with Odin or an earlier incarnation of the chief of the gods. The Yggdrasil Tree was of course known as Odin's

Horse, a euphemism for the gallows. Odin hung from the tree for nine days and nights and was wounded by a spear while he was suspended there, between heaven and earth. We note that nine nights is a multiple of three, of course. These events could easily be commemorated in the strangling and stabbing inflicted upon some of the bodies found in the bogs of Europe. The deposition of the bodies in water would also suggest a dedication to the fertility of the land.

Who would have been responsible for arranging such sacrifices? Almost certainly, this would have been the druids, who were as active in Britain as they were in mainland Europe. They had a stronghold on the Isle of Anglesey, off the coast of Wales. We come now to two curious things which were discovered about Lindow Man, both of which suggest that the druids were involved in his death. The two clues came to light when the contents of the dead man's stomach were examined closely.

About 20 grams of food was recovered from Lindow Man's stomach and gut. Most seemed to be some kind of wholemeal bread or gruel, which had been made from several kinds of cereal, including wheat and barley. One curious circumstance was that some was charred – burned black. There may of course have been a perfectly prosaic explanation for this, maybe his wife just burned the toast that morning! Then again, burned pieces of cake or bread were sometimes used in Europe, until at least the eighteenth century, as a means of drawing lots to see who might be chosen for a sacrifice. Among the Celts, pieces of toasted bread or cake would be placed in a bag, along with one piece which had been burnt black. People would reach into the bag to choose a piece and the unlucky individual who drew the charred portion was the one who would die. This at least is the story as told by more than one Roman historian. In Perthshire in Scotland in the eighteenth century there was a similar tradition at Beltane, more often known as May Day. The person who took out the burned piece was said to be 'devoted', which is to say dedicated to the god and was referred to as being dead. It has been suggested that Lindow Man might have been chose as a sacrificial victim by the same method.

Also among the contents of Lindow Man's stomach and gut were grains of pollen from many plants. One in particular was of interest, which was mistletoe. There are many legends associated with mistletoe and even today, in the twenty-first century, people in Britain hang sprigs of the plant up in their homes at the time of the Winter Solstice. According to Roman writers, the druids had a particular reverence for mistletoe and used to cut it at certain times of the year with sickles made of gold. How true this is, is anybody's guess, but what is certain is that mistletoe was at the very least of some significance to the druids. That pollen from this sacred plant had found its way into Lindow Man's alimentary tract might well indicate that he was in some way connected with some activity associated with druids. If nothing else, the presence of mistletoe pollen made it possible to fix roughly the date of his last meal, for mistletoe flowers in March and April.

There is one more interesting aspect of Lindow Man and that is that he probably belonged himself to the royal of priestly class. His hands showed no signs of any callouses or injuries such as the average agricultural labourer of the time might be expected to display. The nails were neatly filed and the beard trimmed. Whoever he was, he was certainly not the average Iron Age peasant. This reminds us of the sacrifices at which we have already looked at in this book of high-status objects such as swords, shields and helmets. It was thought pleasing to the gods to deliver articles of great value as gifts to them. If one were going to offer up a human sacrifice, then it would be most disrespectful to give them some tramp or random farmworker. The person sent to the gods would more likely have been the best specimen who could be found in the society of the day.

There has always been, in Indo-European tradition, the idea of the king as having both regal and magical authority. In a real sense, kings were sacred. Because of this, the sacrifice of a king was the greatest offering which could possibly be made to the gods. In Ireland, several bog bodies have been unearthed which, like Lindow Man, show every sign of having been aristocratic or kingly. Their hands are well manicured and show no signs of any work. The latest such corpse was found as recently as 2013 in Ireland and this too was assumed, by those working for the national museum, to be either a king or priest-wizard. Like those in England and Denmark, such victims in Ireland had been subjected to the threefold death, being bludgeoned and then strangled, stabbed and sometimes drowned. The sacrifice of king or wizard might be undertaken if a harvest was poor and it was thought that the fertility of the land was failing. It was the responsibility of those in these exalted positions to ensure that crops flourished and weather was not too harsh. If they could not do so, then it might be necessary to sacrifice them and find a new wizard or king.

Before the druids existed as an organized priestly class, there were individuals who guided the population and told them how to go about their lives, whether pastoral or martial. We can be pretty sure that such men were at work in Europe during the Bronze Age. Whether such people would best be described as wizards, priests or even kings is a debatable point. This brings us to something which has been mentioned many times so far, which is the peculiar nature of wizards' headwear according to our modern traditions. Illustration 1 shows the current idea of a wizard's hat.

In 1835 a curious item was discovered near the German town of Schifferstadt. It looked for all the world like a wizard's hat and it was formed of a sheet of gold, ornamented with strange symbols. This object may be seen in Illustration 2. It probably dates from between 1400 and 1300 BC. Ten years later, something rather similar was unearthed not far from Poitiers in France. This one lacked a brim, but otherwise appeared to be very much like the Schifferstadt cone. Since then, two more of these strange things have come to light; all seemingly dating from the Bronze Age. Illustration 2 is of one of these things.

Nobody was quite sure what to make of the four golden artefacts. Were they vases? Phallic symbols? Another suggestion was that they might be caps which were once secured to the top of wooden posts, possibly to mark the boundary of a territory or for another purpose.

That the gold cone from Schifferstadt looked like a hat was thought by many experts to be purely coincidental. However, careful measurement has shown that this is almost certainly the correct explanation. For one thing, the opening at the base of the cones is oval rather than round and is, moreover, just the right size to fit on a human head. Traces of leather have been associated with one of the objects, which suggests that that perhaps they were once lined with leather and held in place by a chinstrap. All the indications are that these really are, or rather were, hats. All are covered with symbols which resemble strongly suns and moons and for this reason they have been tentatively thought to be part of a sun-worshipping cult. It must be remarked at this point that the look of these hats is so remarkably like our idea of what a wizard's headgear should be like, that the resemblance really is startling. Just compare Illustrations 1 and 2!

So far, all we can really say is that somebody in the Bronze Age wore these things on his or her head. We have no idea if this was as part of a special ceremony or whether the person wandered about with one of these on their head during day-to-day life. Wizards? Kings? Priests? The director of the Berlin Museum, where one of the hats ended up in 1996, came up with what seems likely to be the definitive answer to this question. Wilfried Menghin studied the symbols on the hat which the museum owned and came to an astonishing but persuasive conclusion. It had generally been assumed that the concentric circles and moon shapes on the four golden hats were merely decorative flourishes, intended to make the tall hats appear more impressive to Bronze Age peasants, but Menghin thought though that there might be more to it than that.

The circular symbols are arranged in rows, delineated by embossed lines. According to the director of the museum, this was probably a lunisolar calendar, one which would enable dates to be calculated up to 57 months in advance. It would, by counting around the hat, be possible to predict full moons, the spring and autumnal equinoxes and a host of other useful things, all of which would come in very handy for farmers and perhaps even for sailors wishing to know about tides. In place of a written system, the hat in the Berlin Museum could function as a calculator.

The ability to predict what would be taking place in the heavens years in advance would seem like magic to the Bronze Age tribes of Europe 3,000 years ago. No wonder that the folk memory of the man of magic wearing a pointed hat covered with astronomical symbols has lingered on down the millennia. Whether those who wore these hats were kings and queens or merely magicians and fortune-tellers we are never likely to know. What cannot be doubted though is that they would hold positions of great status in society.

Still on the subject of pointed hats, this might be a good time to mention that our images of black-clad witches probably come from a similar source. The druids of Britain and Gaul did not act alone, but had cohorts of female followers to back them up. They are described by the Roman writer Tacitus, when he relates the assault which took place in 60 AD on the druid stronghold on the Isle of Anglesey.

Despite conquering and occupying almost the whole of southern and western Europe, the Romans found that there was still resistance to their rule and they believed that it was organized and led by the druids. Individual chiefs and kings made all sorts of deals with Rome, but the suspicion was that the druids kept people stirred up and were at the back of various rebellions. Rome had a strong grip on Gaul, but the main headquarters of the druids was not there, but rather on an island far away, off the coast of Wales. In 58 AD a new governor was appointed in Britain. Gaius Suetonius Paulinus was determined to bring an end to the activities of the druids and he planned a massive assault on the Isle of Anglesey, or Mona as it was then known. In 60 or 61 AD he assembled a mighty army and headed west into Wales.

No sooner had the governor of the province left London, than restive tribes in south-east Britain decided that this was the perfect time to make a concerted effort to drive out the Roman occupiers once and for all. Leader of the revolt was of course Boudicca, queen of the

Iceni of modern-day Norfolk. She had personal grievances against the Roman army of occupation, but had no difficulty in gathering a large body of followers who were, if the portents were right, prepared to be led in battle against the enemy. Of course, in addition to being a queen, Boudicca was also something of a witch; the two classes went hand in hand at that time and often overlapped. Priest-kings, wizards and witches were all of a piece and, as we have seen, made up one part of the triad of basic classes in both Celtic and Roman society. The druids too were generally drawn from noble families. At any rate, in order to get her army moving towards the nearest Roman city, the town we now call Colchester, Boudicca knew that she would have to give them a sign that at least one of the gods was with them.

The Roman historian Dio Cassius gave an account of Boudicca's actions before Colchester was over-run and put to the torch. That she was acting in a religious capacity or as a seer of the future is plain. She said to her followers;

> 'Let us, therefore, go against them, trusting boldly to good fortune. Let us show them that they are hares and foxes trying to rule over dogs and wolves.' When she had finished speaking, she employed a species of divination, letting a hare escape from the fold of her dress; and since it ran on what they considered the auspicious side, the whole multitude shouted with pleasure, and Boudicca, raising her hand toward heaven, said: 'I thank you, Andraste, and call upon you as woman speaking to woman. I beg you for victory and preservation of liberty.'

Andraste was a goddess to whom Boudicca had earlier made sacrifices. It is very hard to say in what capacity Boudicca was acting during the scene which Dio describes. Was she a priestess? Foretelling the future? What seems certain is that the men upon whom she relied, all accepted that a woman was able to make the appropriate sacrifices and then divine the future course of events. The hare was incidentally a sacred animal to the Celts and using it in this way to indicate what might happen if the army were to mount an assault on a Roman city was a very shrewd move.

While we are thinking of ancient witches, it is good to remember that hares were first brought to Britain by the Celts, during the Iron Age. For the Celts, and quite possibly the Yamnaya, the hare was a sacred animal; one which was associated with magic, divination and enchantments. Hares were often believed to be the familiar animals of witches in later centuries. In 1663 a 70-year-old woman called Julian Cox appeared in court in the Somerset town of Taunton, charged with witchcraft. A hunter gave evidence to the court that he had been chasing a hare with dogs. The contemporary account of the hunter's evidence to the court reads as follows,

> He swore that he went out with a pack of Hounds to hunt a Hare, and not far off from Julian Cox her house, he at last started a Hare. The Dogs hunted her very close, till at last the Huntsman perceiving the Hare almost spent, and making towards a great Bush, he ran on the other side of the Bush to take her up, and preserve her from the Dogs. But as soon as he laid hands on her, it proved to be Julian Cox, who had her head groveling on the ground, and her globes (as he exprest it) upward. He knowing her, was affrighted, that his Hair on his Head stood on end; and yet spake to her, and askt her what brought her there. But she was so far out of Breath, that she could not make him any answer.

The unfortunate old woman was found guilty and hanged four days later. Nor is the belief that witches may sometimes turn into hares an historical curiosity.

In his book *Folk Heroes of Britain*, published in 1982, Charles Kightly relates the story of Boudicca and the hare. He adds, 'Long after Christianisation, indeed, British witches were regularly credited with the power to turn themselves into hares, and as recently as 1969 the author was assured in a remote Lincolnshire village that a local woman still did so.'

Boudicca was not the only woman mentioned by Roman writers when they came to relate the story of the Boudiccan Revolt. The next author at whom we look might shed some light upon our traditional ideas about the appearance of witches. In the Introduction, we considered the fact that we all of us in Europe and North America have a very clear and distinct view of what a witch ought to look like, which is to say clad entirely in black, usually operating at night and almost invariably wearing a tall, black, pointy hat.

While Boudicca was using hares to foretell the future in East Anglia, Suetonius was preparing to break the influence of the druids in Britain and Gaul, once and for all. There were a lot of connections between the people of Britain and those in Gaul and years earlier Julius Caesar had expressed the view that the druids had their base in Britain. After assembling a fleet of flat-bottomed barges to transport parties of infantry, the Romans launched their attack. Together with their boats, cavalry also took part in the operation, the horses swimming across the narrow channel separating Anglesey from the Welsh mainland, with their riders clinging to the bridles and swimming alongside their mounts.

The scene when the Romans reached the shore was an awe-inspiring one. Tacitus, in his *Annals*, tells us what Suetonius found as he and his men tried to establish their beachhead;

> On the beach stood the adverse array, a serried mass of arms and men, with women flitting between the ranks. In the style of Furies, in robes of deathly black and with dishevelled hair, they brandished their torches; while a circle of Druids, lifting their hands to heaven and showering imprecations, struck the troops with such an awe at the extraordinary spectacle that, as though their limbs were paralysed, they exposed their bodies to wounds without an attempt at movement. Then, reassured

by their general, and inciting each other never to flinch before a band of females and fanatics, they charged behind the standards, cut down all who met them, and enveloped the enemy in his own flames.

Two points stand out in this account. The first is that Tacitus should have compared the women associated with the druids to the Furies. The Furies, goddesses of revenge in Greco-Roman mythology, were of course another triad. They were three in number, just like the Fates, the Graces and the Norns of Norse folklore. The second point is that these are women dressed in black, with wild hair and waving flaming torches about. The very image of traditional witches, in other words. It is plain from the context that these fierce creatures were some kind of acolytes of the druids. Were they seers and magicians in training? At any rate, they were women in black with tangled hair, consorting with men who were renowned for foreseeing the future and carrying out sacrifices.

What of that other notable sartorial feature of European witches; the black pointed hat? We saw a plausible way that our ideas about wizards' hats covered in stars and moons might have arisen, but what about the black hats of witches? These are usually shown to be made of softer material that those of wizards, often crumpled a little. Actually, such hats worn by women have been found and they date back thousands of years, to about the same period as Suetonius' assault on the druids of the Isle of Anglesey.

We have looked at the origins of the Indo-Europeans and the way in which their legends and myths were handed down to us. One branch of the tribes of the Indo-Europeans migrated south and east. They moved through what is now Iran, Afghanistan and Pakistan before occupying much of India. It is for this reason that the languages of the Indian subcontinent have recognizable similarities with those of Europe. Another group of tribes headed west into Europe. Until a few decades ago, this was thought to be pretty much the story of the Indo-Europeans. Then, in the early 1970s, a discovery was made which shed an entirely new light on the Indo-Europeans. In China's Taklimakan Desert, which lies between Mongolia and Tibet, some well-preserved mummies came to the attention of Western archaeologists.

The physical conditions of the Taklimakan desert were such as to cause the natural mummification of corpses buried in the ground. The sand was salty, the winters very cold and the summers hot. Above all, there was little moisture to make flesh decay or clothing rot away. The local inhabitants had long known that some bodies which had been dug up were not of Chinese but European appearance. They were tall, the faces lacking the epicanthic eye fold typical of those from East Asia and also they had blond or ginger hair. The textiles in which they were clothed were also atypical of the region; some wore tartan.

The Chinese authorities were not at all enthusiastic at first about seeing the mummies of Europeans found in their territory being publicized and for a while, obstacles were placed in the way of Westerners wishing to investigate. Gradually though, things became easier for archaeologists and carbon dating was undertaken on artefacts found with the bodies. Later, DNA samples were also taken. These confirmed that some 4,000 years ago groups of people of Indo-European origin moved to China, where they settled down and formed a community. Their technology was similar to the tribes of Europe and their clothes were also made in much the same style as the Celts. Because of the very different climatic conditions in Europe though, only fragments of cloth are usually found, rather than the complete sets of clothing of the mummies from the desert.

Some women found in the area excited particular attention. They were uncovered in Subeshi cemetery in the Chinese county of Shanshan and the most noticeable thing about them were the hats which they were wearing when buried. These are tall, conical and made of black felt. They look like nothing so much as a typical witch's hat. As a result, the mummies wearing these strange pieces of headgear were nicknamed the Witches of Subeshi; a name which has stuck. Is it too fanciful to combine the image of the black-clad druids' assistants with the tall black hats of the Indo-Europeans or Celts buried in China and to imagine that they were part of a common female costume? Illustration 3 is of one of the so-called 'Witches of Subeshi'.

We have looked at the possible origins of wizards in Europe as the natural successors to the shamans of the Stone Age. Witches too appear to have been known for thousands of years in Britain, even if they were not referred to as such. Two devices are inextricably linked in our minds with witches and these are cauldrons and wands. Wands are sometimes used by men as well as women, of course, but cauldrons are an essentially feminine accompaniment to the casting of spells. This is strange because although magic cauldrons have an extremely long lineage in the history of European sorcery, it is only in the last few centuries that they have been exclusively associated with women.

Chapter 9

Of Cauldrons and Wands

Two artefacts are linked in our minds with witchcraft. These are of course cauldrons and wands. The cauldron has, since the time of the Tudors at least, been seen as a purely female accoutrement in magical ceremonies. Let us begin though by considering wands, which are freely used by both sexes.

We start by thinking a little about wands and staffs. Long ago, prehistoric people made only that which was of practical use to them. When survival alone is the overriding imperative, there is little to be gained from manufacturing anything which is not of actual use in procuring food or warding off dangerous animals or human enemies. Drawing, painting, sculpture and other artistic endeavours might therefore seem to be fairly pointless from the point of view of staying alive. When we see marvellously realistic paintings on the walls of caves showing horses and buffalo, we ask ourselves why people scraping a living at subsistence level would bother to spend time creating such things. The same applies to axe-heads carved out of semi-precious stone and polished until they gleam, or apparently useless rods of ivory. The answer is that they did so because they thought that there was a practical value in activities like sketching animals on the wall of a cave by the light of a guttering lamp fuelled by animal fat. The purpose was not to set up an art gallery, but rather to enlist the aid of supernatural powers to help feed the tribe. In the same way, 'ornamental' weapons or other artefacts were crafted not to satisfy a creative urge but because they were, to those who made them, as useful as the spears with which they went hunting.

When we come across things such as little statuettes and models made of ivory or chalk, or beautifully-painted pictures of bison on the walls of some old cave, it is tempting to see these as the emergence of our modern desire to create art for art's sake. Perhaps we imagine men and women 15,000 years ago relaxing at the end of a long day hunting mammoths by picking up a paintbrush or carving a six-inch high image in chalk of a nude and clinically obese woman. We would be quite wrong in doing so, because these activities were seen as being at least as vital to the survival and prosperity of the clan as chipping spear points from flint. Our error is caused by the fact that today we have a strict demarcation between religious or magical matters and the everyday business of living. This distinction was wholly lacking until fairly recently in the history of humanity.

In the modern world, we live our lives according to science and commerce. Any dealings with God or supernatural forces are usually leisure activities, taking place for an hour or two in church on a Sunday or at a séance or something of the kind for an evening's diversion. For those who lived more than a few short centuries ago, this would have been a very odd view of reality. The world of devils and angels, together with the spirits of the dead and other forces, were always around them. At times of trouble, people in Europe at one time might cross themselves, mutter a prayer and so on. Enchantments and the evil eye were as real a hazard to crops as a thunderstorm which came just before the harvest was safely gathered in. We are talking now not of the Palaeolithic era but rather Georgian England. In 1751 an old woman in the Hertfordshire town of Tring was suspected by her neighbours of casting spells which harmed cattle. A large mob assaulted Ruth Osborne, the suspected witch, and then threw her in a pond, where she drowned. This took place just 30 miles from London as the Industrial Revolution was poised to begin.

How does all this tie in with magic wands? Paintings and carvings were one means to harness magic for the aid of human endeavours during the prehistoric period. Another was to produce rods or staffs which were made solely for the purpose of endowing an individual with power over the external world. In fiction, we recall how useful

Gandalf's staff proved on many occasions. The present queen of Britain has a ceremonial rod called a sceptre, which symbolizes her power over the realm which she rules. Such staffs, rods or wands have a very long history indeed.

For over a thousand years, between 2000 and 600 BC, people from the Baltic region of North Europe, all the way across to the Ural Mountains, were making wands topped with carved elks' heads. Not only were they producing these strange and seemingly useless objects, they were engraving pictures of their use on rocks; drawings known as petroglyphs. Thirty of these staffs have been found and all are made from antlers. In the petroglyphs they are shown being used in magical ceremonies to subdue animals and aid in hunts. The intact examples were all recovered from graves and it is obvious that they were very personal belongings of certain individuals. One is reminded of the way in which magic wands are seen as being in some sense 'attuned' to their owners. One can hardly imagine anybody but Gandalf being able to make use of his staff or, to give a more modern instance, Harry Potter's wand being used by anybody but he himself. In another fictional example of a wand in action, that of the White Witch in *The Lion, the Witch and the Wardrobe*, her wand is her most powerful weapon and in the climactic battle at the end of the book, it is only when the White Witch's wand is smashed that there is any chance of the battle against her forces being successful.

In addition to the sceptre as a sign of power and authority, ceremonial maces carry much the same connotations. In the House of Commons an ornate mace shows the power of Parliament. Like wands, magical maces which would have been quite impractical in battle have been unearthed from very early times. Like the cave paintings, magic staffs and statuettes, producing a weapon which was of no apparent practical use was not just a way for cavemen to while away the evening after all the work was done! The heads of such maces are often so delicately fashioned that one blow would obliterate all the careful workmanship, but then they were not designed to be used against corporeal targets.

Like the wands made from antlers, they were intended to operate in the realm of spirits, rather than in that of men.

The wizard with his wand has his origins in the shamans of ancient Eurasia. Useless rods and sticks are often found in prehistoric European burials and the most exhaustive examination of these things has yielded no indication that they were ever used for anything at all. Looking closely at tools under a microscope will reveal scratches and marks of wear which are invisible to the unaided human eye, but nothing of the kind may be found on the ivory rods or decorative maces which are dug up.

The so-called 'Red Lady of Paviland' provides a good example of this kind of thing. In 1823 the skeleton of a man was unearthed in South Wales, although the person digging up the bones mistook it for a woman. The body had been anointed with red ochre, a common-enough practice with ancient burials. Within the grave were shells and fragments of a number of rods carved from elephant tusks. We now know that this burial dated back to over 25,000 years to the Palaeolithic Age. What possible use were the ivory rods? None whatever, looked at purely from our modern and materialist perspective.

There can be little doubt that the wands with which we are all familiar have their origins in the objects which have been recovered from these prehistoric burials. They were used in rituals and as symbols of power and sovereignty. So it is today that we are all aware at the back of our minds that no self-respecting wizard or witch could even think of casting a spell without using his or her wand.

We have looked at one of the objects which are traditionally associated with wizards, witches and fairies. It is time now to examine something which, to the modern mind at least, is used only by female sorcerers; that is to say cauldrons. We have Shakespeare to thank for the idea that only witches are likely to possess a cauldron. Just as our ideas of fairies are shaped by their depiction in *A Midsummer Night's Dream*, at which we shall be looking in the next chapter, so too are our notions about witches and cauldrons. Shakespeare's influence on our collective memory runs exceedingly deep. The opening of Act IV of *Macbeth* consists of a scene with which almost any literate person in the West is likely to be familiar, even if he or she has never set foot in a theatre in the whole course of their life. Three witches are dancing around a cauldron, chanting;

> Round about the cauldron go;
> In the poison'd entrails throw.
> Toad, that under cold stone
> Days and nights hast thirty one
> Swelter'd venom sleeping got,
> Boil thou first i' the charmed pot.
> Double, double toil and trouble;
> Fire burn and cauldron bubble.

This then is the archetypal image today of a cauldron and its purpose. Women cast various strange objects into it as it boils and so they weave their magic spells. Most people who have given the matter any thought will probably have concluded that this is just a little artistic licence on Shakespeare's part and cauldrons have not really been used in the past for sorcery or magic.

Before going any further, it might be worth asking ourselves what cauldrons actually are. Cauldrons are really nothing more than large cooking pots with handles at the top so that they may be hung over an open fire. Such receptacles are still used for cooking in parts of Eastern Europe, although they are an increasingly rare sight. The association of cauldrons with magic goes back a very long way, thousands of years before the time of Shakespeare in fact. Magic cauldrons, of the kind which would have been familiar to most people for the purpose of cooking huge amounts of food, featured in a number of ancient legends told by the Celts.

It is from the Celts, a nation who occupied much of Europe before the expansion of the Roman civilization, that most of the stories of magic cauldrons come. It is unlikely though that it was the Celts who invented these tales; they more likely originated with the Yamnaya people and were carried to Europe during the invasions of the Indo-Europeans. One of the most interesting and complete Celtic cauldrons which we possess, that found in Denmark in 1891, is covered in images from a mythology which seems to have more in common with India than it does Europe. This suggests that Celtic cauldrons and the legends in which they feature, are part of an ancient Indo-European tradition, rather than one with its roots in Europe alone.

There were, according to Celtic mythology and legends, different types of magical cauldron. The first, and the one whose origin is easiest to understand, is the Cauldron of Plenty, which always overflows with rich and meaty food. In a society where food was sometimes in short supply and hunger an ever-present threat, it is not hard to see how the idea a magic pot of food which never ran out would have a great appeal. In the hall of a chieftain or king, it would be a mark of his generosity and wealth that unlimited amounts of food and alcoholic drink should be available, enough to satisfy all those present. Both the food and the liquor were dispensed from enormous cauldrons. The word 'enormous' in this context is no exaggeration, as may be seen from an example dug up in Germany in 1979.

Near the village of Hochdorf, in Germany, stood a burial mound dating from the Iron Age. In the 1970s this was excavated to reveal a magnificent tomb, which had been constructed around 500 BC for a man who must have been of considerable importance. He was found lying on a bronze couch of a type never before seen. Next to the couch was a cauldron, made also of bronze and decorated with lions' heads. This vessel had a capacity of 500 litres or over 100 gallons. We know what it was used for, because traces of honey and pollen have been found as a reside at the bottom, which suggests strongly that this great cauldron was filled with the alcoholic beverage known as 'mead'. Mead is made from fermented honey and was very popular with the Celts. It is an incredibly ancient drink, which may easily be seen from the derivation of the word. 'Mead' comes from the Proto-Indo-European word 'Medhu', which means 'sweet drink'. A pot which contained more than 100 gallons of a strong alcoholic drink would certainly seem an inexhaustible source of plenty to the tribe which owned this marvellous article.

Cauldrons full of nourishing broth, containing chunks of meat, would be a feature of large communal feasts. We know this because cauldrons from that time have been found with flesh-hooks, for pulling meat out of the pot. Dagda, a major god in the Irish pantheon, had a mighty cauldron which was always full of meat. This then is the Cauldron of Plenty, one of the main types of cauldrons which we seen in old legends; one founded in the reality of drinking and feasting as a major activity in Europe a couple of thousand years ago.

We come now to the concept of the magical cauldron and the way in which such a thing might still be manifest in the modern world and even now in the twenty-first century fulfilling its old role. This is the Cauldron of Rebirth. It was remarked earlier that religion and magic were at one time all but indistinguishable and we see this clearly when looking at cauldrons. There are many legends about cauldrons as magical objects, but the best example which survives from antiquity is covered in religious, rather than magical, symbolism. Since this ties in with a good deal of what we have earlier been looking at, things such as the fascination of the Indo-Europeans with horned humans, it might be best to begin by looking at the Gundestrup Cauldron.

About 2,000 years ago, craftsmen in what is now southern Bulgaria produced an elaborate vessel, made entirely of silver. About 27in (68cm) wide and 17in (43cm) high, it was a cauldron, decorated with scenes of a religious or magical nature. These portray scenes from an unknown myth cycle. How it found its way from Eastern Europe to Scandinavia, we shall never know, but at some point this magnificent cauldron ended up in what is now the north of modern Denmark. For reasons at which we can only guess, although probably motivated by the same need to bury or throw into water sacrifices at which we have looked, the cauldron was dismantled and concealed in a peat bog. There it lay for many centuries, until in 1891 some men cutting peat came across it. It was named after the place where it was found, Gundestrup.

It must be said at once that we have not the remotest idea what the Gundestrup Cauldron was used for. Such is the nature of the images covering it, it seems unlikely that it was a purely secular object, like a punch bowl or something of that kind. Although this cannot be ruled out, it seems much more likely that the cauldron was religious or magical in nature. This is because it consists of panels showing fantastic images which are very unlikely to be merely the ancient equivalent of fairy tales. In other words, they are not just decorative, but have a deeper meaning.

We have already looked at one of the panels of the Gundestrup Cauldron in an earlier chapter. This is the Lord of the Animals, who may possibly be cognate with the Celtic god Cernunnos and also an Indian deity. This figure has antlers on his head and is attended to one side by a stag with identical antlers. He may be seen in Illustration 10. It will come as no surprise to find that stags appear in another panel. In this one a giant figure, quite possible a god, is holding two stags by their hindquarters. Other figures are more certain to be gods. We have discussed Taranis, the Celtic god who holds a wheel. In the panels of the Gundestrup Cauldron there are a number of men with wheels. Considering the importance of wheels and their role in carrying the Yamnaya from their ancestral homelands and into India and Europe, it is hardly surprising that the wheel should be held in some reverence.

Other images on the Cauldron are more obscure. A woman with a bird, the slaying of bulls, and a man riding on the back of a dolphin. There have been many attempts to tie in the pictures with this or that Irish or Celtic legend, but none of these efforts are impressive. What we can say with some assurance is that the cauldron shows incidents in the affairs of gods and men and that we can perhaps hazard a guess at the names of some of the gods depicted.

What was this particular cauldron used for? Large vessels of about this size are used in a familiar and well-known religion, which is to say Christianity. Catholic and Anglican churches typically contain a large cauldron filled with water, usually with an ornate cover over the top. During certain magical or religious ceremonies, this is removed. The water inside is then splashed on the heads of those who seek admission to the mysteries of the cult. This process, undertaken with water over which a spell has been chanted, is known as baptism. Could the Gundestrup Cauldron have served a similar function? Curiously enough, one of the pictures on the side shows a row of human figures and a gigantic figure, perhaps intended to be a god. This giant is holding a man upside down and looks as he is about to immerse him headfirst in a cauldron. It is not to be supposed that this is offered as a genuine explanation of how the cauldron might really have been used. Rather, it is to draw a parallel with the use of such vessels in today's world. The connection are though quite uncanny when examined closely. Fully to understand this, we need to look at a very old story from Celtic mythology.

Before looking at the story of Bran the Blessed and his cauldron, it is interesting to note how interpretations of matters relating to the ancient world are prone to reflect the society in which they are made. They tell us as much about our own world, in other words, as they do about the Celts or Indo-Europeans. In 1968, a BBC documentary about a recently-discovered body from a Danish bog featured the eminent archaeologist Sir Mortimer Wheeler. Looking at the same panel from the Gundestrup Cauldron which is described above, he claimed that it showed a man having his throat cut and the blood being drained from his body into the cauldron. Nothing of the sort is even remotely discernible in the embossed panel and yet Sir Mortimer spoke with complete assurance, repeating the idea twice, that this image was of a blood sacrifice. Which goes to show that rather than relying upon this or that expert, we should be sure to examine such things for ourselves and make up our own minds about them.

Bran, or Bran the Blessed as he is often known, was a legendary king of Britain. His father was Lyr, the god of the sea. Bran allowed his sister Branwen to marry the Irish king Matholwych. He did not consult Branwen's half-brother Efnisien though and this led to Efnisien causing havoc at the wedding feast. Matholwych and his Irish followers had sailed from Ireland to Wales, which was where Branwen's wedding took place. While all the guests were drinking, singing and feasting, Efnisien crept to where the horses belonging to the Irish were stabled and cut off their lips, ears and tails. When this act of malice was discovered, it not unnaturally led to ill-feeling and the Irish and Britons began fighting. To restore the peace, Bran presented Matholwych with a magic cauldron, which had the power to bring back to life warriors who had been slain in battle. There are shades here though of modern ideas such as zombies, because although the men dipped in this cauldron came back to life, they were unable to speak and were, by implication, without souls. It may be that part of this legend is represented on the Gundestrup Cauldron in the panel which shows a warrior being immersed in a cauldron.

Baptismal fonts were mentioned above as being perhaps analogous with the magical Cauldrons of Rebirth which crop up in Celtic mythology. Baptism of course has a very long history in Christianity, having its origins in the ritual bath of the Mikvah in Judaism. John the Baptist, a cousin of Jesus, instituted the Christian practice of rebirth through being submerged in water. The modern system is, in most churches, a merely symbolic submersion of course, with water taken from a bowl called the font and poured over the head of the individual who is to be 'reborn'. The similarities between the font and the Cauldron of Rebirth are curious though and Christianity has a long and well-documented history of taking over pagan customs and incorporating them into their religious practices. Mention of Christianity brings us neatly to perhaps the most famous cauldron of all, although it is not known by that name. The magic vessel which inspired writers like Mallory and Tennyson was of course called the Holy Grail.

The Holy Grail, or Sangreal as it was also known, was an object of veneration in the medieval period. Many people thought that it was a real thing, although others realized that it was no more than a fanciful invention of poets and storytellers. The tale of the quest for the Grail was hugely popular, because it tied in perfectly with old Celtic stories about magical cauldrons and also entailed an heroic quest, an enduring theme of fiction from the dawn of recorded history. The Grail was described variously as the goblet from which Jesus drank at the last supper or a container which was used to catch his blood when he was being crucified. It had allegedly been brought to Britain by Joseph of Arimathea, in some accounts Jesus' uncle, and then been hidden from sight because the times were so sinful.

It was because of the way that the stories about the Holy Grail echoed so eerily the tales told of magical cauldrons, that the Church did not officially approve of or accept the Grail as being a genuine Christian relic. Its antecedents were too plainly pagan. According to the stories, when the Grail was brought to Camelot, it was covered by a white cloth and yet gave out a pervasive aroma of rich food. So strong was this scent, that all those feasting at the King Arthur's table ate and drank as never before. This makes the Grail sound rather like a Cauldron of Plenty. Later, when Sir Galahad became the only knight pure enough of heart to hold the Grail in his hands and drink from it, he was instantly transported to paradise.

The association of cauldrons with female practitioners of magic, witches, is a little puzzling as none of the legendary cauldrons had anything at all to do with women. Perhaps it is because in real life cauldrons were more likely to be used for cooking than they were the brewing of magic potions and since women did most of the cooking, it was natural to visualize them around a cauldron, rather than men.

One of the things at which we have been looking in this book is the persistence of memory, which is to say the way in which folk memories have been handed down by word of mouth over centuries or millennia. Both cauldrons and wands provide a striking instance of this phenomenon. Toyshops today stock magic wands, aimed primarily at little girls, which often have stars emitting twinkling, coloured lights from them. They are, even in this modern and industrialized society, instantly recognizable as implements of magic. Wands go together with fairies and wizards in the most natural way imaginable. In contemporary culture of course, the wand has in the last 20 years or so reappeared as an icon of magical power. The films made of *The Lord of the Rings* and *The Hobbit* showed the Odinesque figure of Gandalf using his staff or wand to great effect against enemies. The Harry Potter books about a boarding school devoted to wizardry ensures that the rising generation will be inducted into the old ideas about the power of wands, which play an important role in the casting of spells in the cycle of novels.

Cauldrons too have in recent years undergone a cultural revival. Plastic models of cauldrons are now sold for the purpose of children gathering the tribute of sweets when they go Trick and Treating on Halloween. This brings two very old traditions into juxtaposition, for Halloween takes place of course on the same day as the Celtic festival of Samhain. That children should be roaming the streets on this date, some of them wearing tall, pointed black witches' hats and using miniature cauldrons to collect tribute is really quite eerie. It sometimes seems as though the old customs which were part of the Yamnaya myth system are always lurking just below the threshold of our consciousness, just waiting for an opportunity to break forth and once more manifest themselves.

Chapter 10

On the Nature of Fairies

Ask people today to describe fairies and you are very likely to be given a description of something similar to Tinkerbell from the book *Peter Pan*. A cute little thing about 6in high, wearing a white dress and with delicate, gossamer wings. Typically, such a being would be about the size of a Barbie doll. In short, something which would not look out of place perched on top of a Christmas tree. This idea of fairies, widespread and common though it is, dates only from the seventeenth century. Shakespeare is partly to blame. The sweet little creatures in *A Midsummer Night's Dream*, with whimsical names like Cobweb and Mustardseed, have had a great effect on our subconscious mind. This idea of fairies as cute little girls grew to fruition in the Victorian era and by the dawn of the twentieth century, the image was firmly established. When, in 1917, two young girls set out to produce supposedly authentic photographs of fairies, they naturally thought that their productions should be no more than 6in high and with translucent wings. Fairies and elves, in this version of the myth, were essentially good-natured and exceedingly tiny people, who might at worst play mischievous tricks on unsuspecting humans. Fairies were of course almost invariably female, which explains why the word was used in a pejorative sense at one time as a term for male homosexuals.

These ideas about the Little People would have seemed quite bizarre to anybody living in Europe before about 1600. Up to that time, and for centuries later in more remote and isolated parts, fairies were feared and respected in equal measure. That they existed was beyond question and fairies were seen as being as much a hazard of forest and moorland as wolves and bears. A passage in *Jane Eyre*, written of course by a young woman living in a fairly remote part of Yorkshire in the early nineteenth century, gives some idea of how the Little People were still seen in rural areas at that time. It will be recalled that Mr Rochester's first encounter with the new governess comes when she is walking to post a letter and his horse slips on ice, throwing the rider. Rochester pretends to think that Jane Eyre is a fairy and later that day the following conversation takes place;

> 'And so you were waiting for your people when you sat on that stile?'
> 'For whom, sir?'
> 'For the men in green: it was a proper moonlight evening for them. Did I break through one of your rings, that you spread that damned ice on the causeway?'

One thing which we at once pick up from this snatch of dialogue is that the Little People are not viewed in a very favourable light. Legends lingered on that fairies and elves could be dangerous if humans crossed their path unwittingly or uninvited. Although an educated man like Mr Rochester would not actually subscribe to such beliefs, he is certainly aware of them. Note too that he does not refer directly to fairies or elves, but instead uses the allusive 'men in green'. This too was part of a very old tradition. They were seldom spoken of, other than in terms of great politeness, lest they be eavesdropping upon conversations. It was considered unwise to name them out loud and a taboo was attached to words such as 'elf' or 'fairy'. They were instead referred to by a variety of euphemisms; 'the good people' or 'the hidden folk', for instance. If fairies were mentioned by name, it was considered wise to add, 'Bless them!' Angering them could lead to all sorts of evil consequences, up to and including the snatching a baby from its crib. It was dangerous to fall out with the Little People, and Rochester hints jokingly that he thinks that causing offence to them might have precipitated the fall from his horse.

Fairies, elves, pixies, dwarves, brownies and leprechauns appear throughout European folklore and although at first sight the various races appear different, they have certain common characteristics which might allow us to make a few shrewd guesses about their origins. We saw in an earlier chapter that the eponymous central character in the folktale *Rumpelstiltskin*, the eponymous central character of which may be seen in Illustration 7, is one of the Little People and since this story probably dates back at least 3,000 years, it is obvious that such beings have been in our minds for almost as long as civilization in Europe has existed.

The first and most immediate thing which we observe about oldest tales of fairies is that they interact with the real world. In other words, they are not ghosts, angels or insubstantial spirits. This needs to be mentioned, because all three explanations have in the past been advanced to account for the legends about fairies. They can affect their surroundings physically and are able to talk to and hear humans. The next noticeable feature is the size of the so-called 'Little People'. They are not tiny, the size of dolls. Certainly, they are smaller than the average human, but are at least as big as children, usually bigger. They are like stunted or very small humans. Some of the Little People, brownies for instance, are explicitly described as being dark-skinned and having a lot of hair on their bodies. Mr Rochester talked of 'the men in green' and this draws our attention to another point, that fairies almost invariably dress in green or brown. They avoid bright colours. Some wear little more than rags and go about half naked.

What relations do the fairies or Little People have with us? This is not an easy question to answer. Perhaps the most sinister aspect of their dealings with humans is the indisputable fact that they seem to crave human babies. The entire plot of *Rumpelstiltskin* of course revolves around a plan to acquire a human baby, as does *Rapunzel*. There is too the recurring theme of the 'changeling'. This is the idea that the fairies would steal away babies, usually those who had not yet been baptised, and substitute one of their own babies for the human child. The changeling, for so it was called, was invariably a sickly, wizened creature. A number of old stories tell how the baby could be regained and the changeling returned to its own people.

The Little People sometimes undertook tasks around homes and farms, in exchange for gifts of food, typically dairy produce. At other times, they would steal food and tools from families living in isolated areas. Cows would be milked dry, orchards raided and portable objects like spades or sickles stolen. Then there were bits of minor vandalism, which the victims often understood to have been acts of spite carried out because they had spoken disrespectfully of the Little People or failed to make the correct offerings to them. From time to time, stone arrowheads would be turned up when ploughing and these were associated with the fairies. They were called 'elf-bolts' by country folk. The belief was that elves had fired flint-tipped arrows at those working in the fields.

To go off at a slight tangent, in rural districts fairies were blamed for almost anything which broke or went missing. If a farm tool or implement could not be found, people might remark, 'It's those blessed fairies!'. Sometimes this was done half humorously, but also it was honestly believed that from time to time the Little People would make off with something useful. This whole scenario formed the basic premise of a hugely successful series of children's books by the author Mary Norton. The Borrowers were a family of, quite literally, little people, who lived beneath the floorboards of a large house. They raided the home belonging to the humans for anything they required, things such as needles and thread. This theft was disguised by the euphemism of 'borrowing'. The first book in this series, *The Borrowers*, won the 1952 Carnegie Medal for the most outstanding children's book of the year.

Just as *The Lord of the Rings* appealed to the subconscious awareness of a forgotten world and so became popular, in the same way *The Borrowers* appealed to half-remembered myths which tugged at the memories of those reading it. That this was wholly subconscious may be seen from the way in which those analysing the book's appeal seemed unable to see the relevance of the story of the little people stealing the belongings of humans in anything other than modern metaphors. The author A.N. Wilson suggested that the story was an allegory of life in post-war Britain, with the small people living in a run-down old mansion as being symbolic of Britain in the years following the end of the Second World War. The actual source of the story and its attraction altogether eluded him.

What are we to make of all this? For all the later legends which accumulated about the fairies, there does not seem to be anything in the earliest stories to indicated much that was supernatural about them. It is true that some could weave spells, but then so could some humans, wizards for example. All that we know of them from the very earliest stories suggest that they are limited and restricted by the same rules as ordinary humans. Gravity holds them to the ground, they need to eat and drink and they communicate not through telepathy or anything of that kind, but by speaking and listening just the same as anybody else.

Wearing green clothing or brown makes it sound almost as though the 'hidden people' were adopting camouflage colours to make them less conspicuous as they moved about the countryside. Why should they wish to steal tools and so on from farms? What is it with the Little People that they should have it in mind to get hold of human babies? The overall impression one gains is that fairies and elves lived in communities which were separate from those of humans, but were perfectly able to interact with the material world. They could pick things up to steal them, for instance, not something that any ghost could do. And if they were the spirits of dead humans, as some have hypothesized, what could they possibly want with the farm implements which they made off with from time to time? What use would an axe be to a ghost?

Here is a fable, or tentative account, which might perhaps offer a non-supernatural explanation for the origin of fairies and elves. About 5,000 years ago Europe, including Britain, was home to a race of short, dark-skinned farmers. These Neolithic people had no metals and lived largely by subsistence farming, supplementing their crops by fishing, hunting and the gathering of wild berries, mushrooms and so on. They were small and wiry because for much of the time they lived more or less on the edge of starvation. These aboriginal inhabitants of Europe spoke dozens, perhaps hundreds, of different languages, just as in New Guinea today there are many mutually unintelligible languages, with people unable to understand even those living a few miles away in the next valley.

Around 2500 BC, the quiet life of these Neolithic farmers was overturned as invaders from the east surged across the continent. The newcomers had wagons and metal swords, against which the flint weapons of the indigenous inhabitants were useless. All they could do was make hit-and-run attacks against the marauding tribes. These people were taller, stronger and paler than those living in Europe. They were bigger because they were better nourished. They drove their herds of cattle and sheep with them as they travelled. This provided them with a protein-rich diet of dairy products and meat, rather than the thin gruel made of wheat and barley which was the staple diet of the Europeans.

As the years passed, the Yamnaya, for it was they and their descendants who were sweeping in from the steppes, consolidated their grip upon the continent and established their own settlements. They disposed ruthlessly of the men they encountered, putting them to the sword, but some of the women they allowed to become slaves and concubines. Slowly, but inexorably, the original inhabitants of the land withdrew into the forests and mountains. There, they eked out a wretched existence, making guerrilla raids on those who had stolen their land. Sometimes they would fire flint-tipped arrows at men working in the fields. Hunger drove them to desperate action such as sneaking into barns at night and milking cows dry or stealing as much fruit from an orchard as they could carry away. For obvious reasons, these resistance fighters ensured that their clothes would not stand out at a distance. They dressed in material which had been dyed green with plant material and they would cover themselves in sprigs of heather, twigs and leaves, in an attempt to blend into the landscape. This led superstitious countrymen to mistake them for nature spirits.

As the bands of those who fought back against the usurpers dwindled in size, inbreeding took place, cousin marriages or even coupling between brothers and sisters. This led to genetic defects and the birth of sickly and deformed babies. To improve their own stock, those who were now known as the 'hidden people' would sometimes find a way to exchange one of their own sickly babies for a robust and healthy one belonging to the invaders.

As time passed, some of those in hiding gave up and came to work as servants for the new owners of the land. These small, stocky and dark-skinned men became known as 'brownies' and they worked around farms in exchange for food. Those who maintained the struggle, however, would come at night and take the metal tools which they were unable to make themselves. The question of metal is an interesting one for the Yamnaya were keenly aware that it was their mastery of smithing which had given them the edge over those who had once lived where they did. So it was that a piece of folklore arose that iron provided protection against fairies.

As the decades became centuries and eventually millennia, the history of the invasion and occupation of Europe became forgotten. All that was recalled was that a small people had once lived here and could still be glimpsed from time to time. It was considered taboo to speak aloud of these little ones and so a number of euphemisms were devised, such as the 'good people'. This hidden race could cause problems if one was not careful to placate them with gifts of food. They were quite capable of wreaking havoc at night and playing mischievous tricks. Although they seldom did so these days, at one time they fired arrows with stone points at people and these would sometimes turn up in ploughed fields.

It is of course impossible at this late stage, 4,000 years or more after the event, to say whether or not this scenario provides a real explanation for the stories which we have today about fairies and elves, but it does seem to cover most of the known facts. Looking at what we know of the world of the fairies certainly suggests a Neolithic origin, rather than a society from the Bronze Age or later. Fairies did not appear to have domestic animals or to ride horses. They did not use the wheel either and were distinctly opposed to the presence of metal. They existed in a state of, if not hostility towards, then at the very least suspicion towards humans. It was plain that relations between the Little People and the human race were tense and could erupt into open animosity at times. The best way of summing up the case, looking at old legends, is to say that a watchful truce existed between the two communities and it was generally agreed that it was best if both kept their distance from the other.

Is it conceivable that folk memories could preserve events which had taken place thousands of years earlier in the way which is described above? Is it possible that stories could be handed down in this way over a hundred generations or more? We have seen a few examples of this happening, now let us look at two more cases, one of which involves stories of 'little people'.

Most of us are familiar with the Biblical story of Noah's Flood, when the whole earth was supposedly inundated with water, leaving only Noah and his family alive. It will be remembered that they built a ship, known as the Ark, onto which they loaded livestock and so rode out the deluge. In 1872 the Assyriologist George Smith addressed a public meeting in London at which he read out a similar version of this story, which he had translated from a cuneiform tablet from around 2000 BC. It seemed that the story of the great flood was a common one across the Middle East.

The narratives about the flood dated from 2000 or 3000 BC and yet there was, until 1993, no archaeological evidence for such an event. True, there had been localized flooding from the Euphrates overflowing its banks during the rainy season, but this was hardly a catastrophic occurrence.

Since few people today believe in a literally worldwide flood and evidence of such a thing cannot be found in the Middle East, some researchers began looking a little further afield for some dramatic climatic change which could have led to the legends of the Great Flood. They found it in the area which today lies between Turkey, Russia, Ukraine and Bulgaria, the stretch of water known as the Black Sea. The geology of the area made it likely that what is now the Black Sea was once a large, shallow depression of fertile land surrounding a freshwater lake. This oasis was separated from the Mediterranean Sea by a ridge of land in what is now Istanbul. This rocky prominence acted, in effect, as a dam, preventing the waters of the Mediterranean from cascading down into the valley below.

When the last Ice Age came to an end, the melting icecaps and glaciers ran into the ocean, raising the sea level across the whole world. As the level of the Mediterranean rose inexorably, pressure began to build on the tongue of land separating the area of the Black Sea from the rest of the Mediterranean. By now, the communities living on the shores of the lake in that warm and comfortable land were some 500ft (142m) below sea level. Disaster was imminent. It arrived 7,500 years ago, when the dam finally burst and the Mediterranean began pouring over what is now the Bosporus in what was one of the mightiest waterfalls ever seen. It was the equivalent of 200 Niagara Falls. Within a year, 60,000 square miles of land had been inundated and the freshwater lake and surrounding country was submerged to a depth of 500ft in seawater.

The sequence described above was confirmed in 1993 when two marine biologists from Columbia University in the United States took samples from the seafloor in the part of the Black Sea close to the Ukrainian coast. William Ryan and Walter Pitman found freshwater mollusc shells, the roots of land plants and other signs that dry land had once existed hundreds of feet beneath the surface of the sea. Six years later an expedition sent down remote-controlled cameras and found beaches, headlands and more freshwater shells. These were dated to 5500 BC.

Of course, those immediately in the path of that torrential waterfall would have been swept away and killed at once. But for those further away, the water would have risen and advanced at a rate of about a kilometre a day, plenty of time for people to gather up their belongings and flee to higher ground. Perhaps some built rafts on which some livestock might have been loaded, possibly a few goats and sheep. The sudden flooding of an area of warm ground in this way may well have precipitated extreme weather, heavy rain and thunderstorms, say.

This is all a far cry from the universal deluge and a boat the size of a modern ocean-going liner that we read of in the Bible, but then it happened 3,000 years before the invention of writing. Some of those refugees fleeing from what must have seemed like the end of their world would have ended up in what is now Turkey, from where they could have carried their stories of the flood to Babylon and Assyria. It seems highly likely that these stories were passed down by word of mouth before finally being set down in cuneiform 4,000 years ago

The second example of what might be a long-lived folk memory concerns the people on the island of Flores in Indonesia. The Nage people who live on Flores have legends about a race of little people whom they call the Ebu Gogo. According to myth, these people are about a metre and a half tall and live in the forest. They are very primitive and their spoken language sounds like the noises which animals make. So backward are the Ebu Gogo culturally that they have not mastered the use of fire, eating all their food raw. In the Nage language, Ebu Gogo means something like 'old person who eats anything'. This small race are apparently very swift runners, good at hiding and have hairy bodies. There are stories, eerily similar to those told by the Indo-Europeans, about the Ebu Gogo kidnapping small children. There are obvious parallels here with the story of the changeling. In the fairy tales of the Nage, the children who are captured in this way are taken because the

Ebu Gogo want know the secret of fire and cooking. Because they are so slow-witted though, the children always manage to trick them and escape back to their families. There are echoes here of course with the familiar story of Hansel and Gretel.

The stories about the Ebu Gogo which Westerners heard over the years were generally assumed to be garbled versions of the dealings which monkeys had over the years had with the Nage. Flores is a large and populous place, almost two million people living on the island, but much of it is wild and unexplored. In 2003 archaeologists digging in a limestone cave came across something remarkable. It was the partial skeleton of an archaic human, belonging to a species which had lived before the coming of *Homo sapiens* or modern humans. The remarkable thing about this discovery was that although clearly an adult, this was somebody who would have stood little more than 3ft high, about half the height of people today. Since this discovery was made midway through the release of the trilogy of films based on Tolkien's *The Lord of the Rings*, it was perhaps inevitable that this tiny person should be nicknamed 'the hobbit'. This name has stuck.

It was at first speculated that this discovery on Flores might be an atypical individual with some kind of disability, perhaps microcephaly combined with something else. Since then though the remains of nine individuals have been found, all of the same height. The most plausible explanation is that these are a descendent of *Homo erectus*, the first human species to spread across the world. A community finding itself isolated on Flores might have succumbed to what is known as 'island dwarfism'. This happens when a population of animals becomes restricted to a certain habitat and grows gradually smaller over the years.

There is some debate about when the 'hobbits' of Flores died out, but it was certainly after the arrival of modern humans, whose descendants now live there, 40,000 years ago. In light of these recent findings, the idea has been mooted that the stories about the Ebu Gogo might be rooted in real memories of the little people who lived on the island before the bigger humans landed there. It is being suggested that the Ebu Gogo legends are folk memories of the sort at which we have been looking. Similar questions have been asked about the Orang Pendek, about which stories have circulated for years in parts of Indonesia. In the language of Indonesia Orang Pendek means 'short person' and is supposed to be a bipedal ape which walks the forests. Could this too be a folk memory of the earlier inhabitants? Recent research in the field of phylogenetic analysis of folk tales suggests that this is indeed possible.

If it is true that some fairy tales today were circulating in oral form 6,000 years ago, before the Yamnaya tribes began moving out of their ancestral homeland, then it is far from implausible that others of which we know could have their origins just 4,000 or 5,000 years ago. If true, and there is every reason to suppose that this is the case, then it shows with startling clarity just how long such oral traditions may last. These stories were not actually written down until about 500 years ago, which means that for thousands of years they were circulating by word of mouth, being told around the hearth or to children as they lay in bed before going to sleep.

This slight diversion into the idea of folk memories has been necessary to provide some background for the apparently extraordinary idea that stories of what happened during the Yamnaya invasions of India and Europe might have survived in distorted and embroidered forms down to the present day. Specifically, it is suggested that the stories of fairies, elves and goblins might be such folk memories, albeit grossly exaggerated, of the interactions between the Indo-Europeans who settled in Europe and the indigenous inhabitants of that continent, who were all but wiped out. This would have happened between 5,500 and 3,500 years ago. The stories of *Rumpelstiltskin* and *Beauty and the Beast* fall well within this timeframe.

What this means is that a story like *Rumpelstiltskin*, in which a member of a hidden race with unknown and mysterious powers tries to acquire a human baby, could easily be part of the mythos surrounding the so-called 'Little People'. The idea of fairies wanting to carry away a human baby may well be based upon and inspired by things which really happened 4,000 years or so ago.

It has to be said that this explanation of the origins of legends about fairies is not universally accepted; there are two other chief explanations, both of which were touched upon briefly above. One is that the fairies represent the spirits of the dead and the other that they are really nature spirits, the elemental life forces of trees or streams. Neither of these hypotheses is entirely convincing. If the fairies are no more than ghosts, then why would they go to the trouble of raiding orchards or milking cattle dry? What use would they have for apples or milk? Similarly, if they were supposedly entities such as dryads or other nature spirits, why would they need green clothes to camouflage themselves? Why would people have assumed that flint arrowheads had been fired by elves?

That the fairies were in reality flesh and blood beings seems reasonably clear from a close examination of the legends surrounding them. That ordinary mortals were afraid of them or at least viewed them with considerable respect is also certain. We know that there was the apprehension that the 'good folk' or 'hidden people' could inflict physical harm, by stealing or sabotaging farming equipment, for example. They were also quite capable of kidnapping babies. None of these are activities commonly carried out by ghosts.

There remains, however, the undeniable fact that fairies were regarded as skilled practitioners of magic. Some cast spells and enchantments and could cause all manner of mischief in this way. Here too, the possibility that they were the remnants of an earlier ethnic group, overwhelmed and all but obliterated by the arrival of tribes from the Yamnaya homeland, fits in very neatly with the traditional beliefs about fairies.

Much of this book has been concerned with the ideas which the descendants of the Yamnaya brought to Western Europe 5,000 years ago. Some of these ideas though were hardly novelties to the peoples whom they supplanted. As we have seen, a preoccupation with horned animals such as deer and rhinoceros even pre-dates the emergence of our own human species. Such things run very deep in the psyche of all humans. The examples of the headdresses with antlers from Yorkshire and the cave painting from the French site of Trois-Frères show that such traditions of magic were flourishing in Europe 10,000 years before the arrival of the Yamnaya.

They might have seen themselves as the future, thoroughly up-to-date and modern people who wielded metal weapons, travelled on wheeled wagons or rode on domesticated horses, but even as they committed genocide against the farmers and nomads who they encountered, the Yamnaya knew that their victims were the inheritors of very old knowledge and traditions. Modern DNA analysis shows that the Yamnaya themselves came originally, at least in part, from Europe. They were the descendants of hunter-gatherers who had wandered east into what is now Ukraine at some distant time in the past and settled in a new part of the world. Not unnaturally, they took with them the religious or supernatural customs of the Europe which they were quitting. On one level, psychologically, they recognized perhaps that those whose lands they were seizing were practitioners of the oldest form of their own magic and religion.

One of the fascinating things about myths is that they have a habit of mutating and being adapted to new circumstances as the years past. It would have greatly surprised the Yamnaya settlers had they known that within a few thousand years, they themselves would have been regarded as the Little People! Nevertheless, it was to be the case. This new version of the legend of the Little People is, astonishingly, still going strong in parts of the British Isles.

In the Introduction it was remarked that old stories about wizards, witches and fairies have a tendency to linger on in parts of Europe which are on the very edge of the continent. This happened in Scandinavia, partly because the peninsula which comprises Norway and Sweden is separated from mainland Europe by an arm of the Baltic Sea. This means that tales of goblins and trolls are still current there in more remote country districts. It is also in the so-called 'Celtic Fringe' though that belief in fairies and fear of their supernatural powers has outlasted not only the Industrial Revolution, but even the advent of computers and smartphones.

The Celtic Fringe is the outermost parts of the British Isles in the west, which provided a refuge for the Celts and later Romanised Britons who fled the encroachment of the Angles, Saxons and Jutes who invaded Britain after the fall of the Roman Empire. This is why Welsh and Gaelic have remained living languages in those places. Cornwall is also part of the Celtic Fringe. Separated from the rest of the country by the River Tamar, Cornwall was practically an island until a few centuries ago. It is in those places, Ireland, Wales, the western coast of Scotland and Cornwall that belief in fairies lasted longest.

Returning to the idea that the Indo-Europeans who settled in Europe 4,000 or 5,000 years ago would one day come to be associated themselves with fairies, there are in Ireland and Cornwall locations known as 'fairy forts'. These are ringforts, the remains of circular fortified homesteads, the oldest of which date back to the Bronze Age. Often, all that remains of these structures is a ditch and bank, which once protected a farmhouse or hamlet. Drystone walls would typically have surmounted the bank and the family or families would have their homes within the circle. The remnants of most of these old dwellings are to be found in Ireland, but Cornwall and Wales also boast a few. Over the years the myth arose that these places are either former strongholds of, or entrances to the world of, the Little People.

In Cornwall, the connection of the fortified settlements with the fairies is reinforced by the mysterious, man-made caves known as fogous. A few are also to be found in Scotland, most notable on the Orkney Isles. These short tunnels are built of drystone walling and then covered with earth. The reason for the construction and the purpose which they served are quite unknown today. However, it was once thought that the world of the fairies was underground and could only be reached through caves or deep holes and for this reason, the fogous found near the fairy forts supported the idea that such remains had originally been the homes of the Little People. Superstitious country folk in Cornwall, and especially in Ireland, would give fairy forts a wide berth, lest they be carried off into the land of the fairies. It was thought to be very unlucky to tamper with, harm or attempt to remove these structures and farmers preferred to utilize them for agricultural purposes rather than to risk harm by damaging them in any way. Some, for example, were used as enclosures for livestock. So powerful were the superstitions surrounding fairy forts that as late as 1895, they resulted in a ritual murder being committed in Ireland.

In 1887 18-year-old Bridget Boland married a barrel-maker called Michael Cleary. The couple were both born and raised in the Irish county of Tipperary and it was only natural that it was in that part of Ireland that they should set up home after their marriage. They lived in the little town of Ballyvadlea. Bridget was very interested in fairies, which was not thought to be healthy at that time. She walked around the area selling eggs and on a nearby hill stood a fairy fort, which everybody else avoided, especially after dark. Bridget though would go out of her way to pass through the place and liked to linger there at dusk. This caused raised eyebrows. Nor was this her only connection with the Little People. Her father became ill and needed to be looked after. There was not room in their home, but because Patrick Boland, her father, had once been a labourer, it was arranged that they could move into a cottage which was specially reserved for labourers and their families. This was one of the best houses in the village, but nobody else wanted to live there because it had been built on the site of another fairy fort and was therefore seen as being an unlucky place to spend the night.

The marriage between Michael Cleary and his wife Bridget proceeded without any great problems for eight years. The couple did not have any children, but apart from that there seemed little to distinguish them from any other working-class family in Tipperary at that time. On 4 March 1895 Bridget Cleary walked over to her cousin's farm to deliver some eggs. It was a cold day, with snow on the ground, and she unwisely made a detour to visit the fairy fort on Kylenagranagh Hill. She came home late, and the next day was in bed with a chill.

Bridget was ill for the next week and it was during that time that her husband became gripped by the genuine belief that the woman lying in bed was not actually his wife at all, but a changeling. He honestly thought that his wife had been carried off by the fairies and that they had sent a substitute who looked very similar to Bridget, but was not exactly like her. For instance, he claimed that the woman now in his house was two inches taller than his wife. Other relatives and friends agreed and hatched a plan to force the imposter to reveal herself. The sick woman was asked three times by Cleary to answer to the question, 'Are you Bridget Boland, wife of Michael Cleary, in the name of God?' She stumbled on answering the third time, which was seen as a sign that she was not the genuine woman.

After 11 days, Bridget Cleary was well enough to get up and asked for some milk. This aroused her husband's suspicions again, because fairies were famous for having a liking for fresh milk; that's why they sometimes milked cows dry in the night. There were a number of other people in the house, which made what happened next all the more shocking. Having, as he saw it, strong evidence that the woman in his home was really a changeling, a fairy trying to pass as human, Michael Cleary knocked her to the ground and grabbed a burning stick from the fire, which he held close to her mouth. Then he set fire to her clothes and, to make absolutely sure of the result, he poured lamp oil over his wife. She blazed like a torch. There were cries of horror from some of those present, but not one person attempted to help the burning woman and she soon died. Even her own father did nothing to save her.

After burying her in a shallow grave, Michael Cleary spent the next few days haunting the ringfort at on Kylenagranagh Hill. He was convinced that now he had disposed of the fairy who was impersonating his wife, Bridget would return to him, riding on a white horse. After three days though, not only had his wife not returned to him but the police had heard some disturbing rumours. Michael Cleary and a number of other men were arrested and charged with wounding. Cleary was additionally charged with manslaughter. By this time, the dead woman's remains had been found.

It was ruled in court that murder was not a possibility because Michael Cleary genuinely believed that the person whom he was burning to death was not human. He was sent to prison for 20 years. Others who had been involved in the death received sentences ranging from six months to five years imprisonment with hard labour. To this day, children in that part of Ireland recite a nursery rhyme inspired by the dreadful events,

> Are you a witch or are you a fairy,
> Or are you the wife of Michael Cleary?

There is something ironic about the Indo-European invaders regarding earlier inhabitants of the land as fairies, only for later generations to view them and their works in that same light. The above case illustrates perfectly how those who really believe in fairies feel about them. There is nothing cute and mischievous about the Little People; they are a deadly menace. It may seem incredible, but these ideas have not yet died out, at least in Ireland.

In 1992 Sean Quinn was the richest man in Ireland. He owned hotels, quarries and a large cement business. That year, he wished to extend a quarry he owned, but a 4,000-year-old megalithic tomb stood in his way. His company, Quinn Cement, obtained permission from the Office of Public Works to dismantle the tomb and it was relocated in the grounds of an hotel owned by Quinn. Then his business problems began and they culminated in the richest man in Ireland being declared bankrupt. Local people were in no doubt that it was the revenge of the fairies upon a man who had disturbed one of their haunts.

Chapter 11

How Christianity made Wizardry Disreputable

Attention has been drawn throughout this book to the similarity between the Devil of Christian mythology and some of the oldest visual images of gods in Europe and south Asia. In particular the horns and cloven feet put us in mind of Cernunnos, the Lord of the Animals, the figure on the Gundestrup Cauldron and a host of other paintings and sculptures dating back at least 15,000 years. It can hardly be a coincidence that our modern Devil has somehow acquired these characteristics. Not only has a very old and respected god been transformed into the chief of all demons, other fellow deities have been hijacked by Christians and co-opted into serving the religion as saints. At the same time, wizards, witches and seers, all honourable occupations for thousands of years, find themselves being associated with the powers of darkness and liable to suffer horrible deaths for their traditional practices. To understand what happened, we need to look at religions in general and then at Christianity in particular.

Europe, Iran and Northern India all have a common cultural heritage, dating from the time that the descendants of the Yamnaya settled in those places 4,000 or 5,000 years ago. This means that the gods worshipped by the Romans and Greeks, Celts and Norsemen and also those of the Hindus, all derive from very ancient originals. These templates were formed in prehistoric Eastern Europe. This is most clearly seen when we compare the Roman gods and goddesses with those of Greece. In Proto-Indo-European, the language which the Yamnaya spoke, there was a name for their supreme god, the king of the gods, if you will. He was known as the 'Sky Father'. In their language, this was 'Dyeus Pate'. We recognize at once the word 'pater', which we known means 'father' in Latin. It is the root of the English word 'paternal', meaning fatherly.

From this original term for the chief of the gods, we see the Sanskrit 'Dyaus Pita', which is almost identical. In Latin, this became 'Ju Piter' and in archaic Greek, 'Zeu Pater'. From these phrases we see how the Roman Jupiter and the Greek Zeus were really no more than different words for the same important god. We have no written record of the names which the Celts gave to the deities which corresponded to those of Greece and Rome, for they were not a literate people. Instead, we must rely upon what men like Julius Caesar wrote about them.

In *The Gallic Wars*, Caesar described the gods worshipped by the Gauls, who were of course Celts. He used the Roman names for them, but clearly recognized that they were essentially the same pantheon which he himself held in high regard,

> Of the gods, they worship Mercury above all. There are numerous images of this god, they speak of him as the founder of all skills and the guide of roads and routes, they regard him as having very great power over financial profits and trade. In second place they worship Apollo, Mars, Jupiter, and Minerva, and they have more or less the same view of these deities as other peoples have that: Apollo drives away illnesses, Minerva institutes arts and crafts, Jupiter has the rule of the gods and Mars regulates wars.

This meant that wherever they went in Europe, the Romans made no attempt to stamp out the indigenous religion and impose their own. In their dealings with the Celts, they accepted that they were all worshipping the same gods under different names. Taranis, for instance, the 'thunderer', was identified by the Romans as being the same as their Jupiter, the ruler of the gods. Teutates was seen as being Mars, the god of war, under a different guise. A consequence of this was the establishment in Britain and other parts of Europe under the Roman occupation, of what we now call Romano-Celtic temples. These were places of worship which could be used as easily by a Roman soldier as they could be by a British or Gaulish merchant. Typically, they might be known by the dual name of the Roman and Celtic gods. At the English town of Bath are the remains of a temple dedicated to Sulis-Minerva. Sulis was a Celtic goddess whom the Romans thought was their own Minerva in another guise and so the names were combined to provide one place of worship which would be convenient for everybody living in the area.

This easy-going and relaxed attitude to the gods of others is of course the antithesis of the Christian view of religion. So too was the view of Christianity bitterly and diametrically opposed to the priests and prophets of other religions, which has a direct bearing on the view of witches and wizards which has been passed down to us from the medieval period onward.

Not only did the Romans tolerate the gods of the Celts, they were also content to let their prophets and priests alone, at least as long as they did not try to stir up rebellion. We have touched on the general tendency of cultures which derived from the Yamnaya to recognize three chief elements in their societies, which equate roughly to priests, warriors and peasants. The Celts, like the Romans, Greeks and Indians, adhered to this tripartite division and the Greek geographer Strabo wrote of them that,

> Among all the tribes, generally speaking, there are three classes of men held in special honour: the Bards, the Vates and the Druids. The bards are singers and poets; the Vates interpreters of sacrifice and natural philosophers; while the Druids, in addition to the science of nature, study also moral philosophy.

In addition to these three groups, who might all fall broadly under the category of priests, Strabo mentioned also the farmers and knights.

The Vates, those whom Strabo described as interpreting sacrifices, were seers and magicians. They foretold the future and claimed to know what the gods required of men. Some of this class were men, but certain women too could take on this role. We saw how Boudicca engaged in prognostication, reading in the direction which a freed hare ran an indication of military victory.

Christianity and the god whom Christians worship have always been very different from the relaxed and laid-back polytheism which was one legacy of the Yamnaya. For one thing, the god of the Christians was very much the Jewish god, who was explicitly stated to be a 'jealous' god; one who could brook no rivals. The whole narrative of the Old Testament is the struggle of their prophets and leaders to save Israel from the deplorable tendency to slip into polytheism at the drop of the proverbial hat. The first of the Ten Commandments removes all doubt about the importance of avoiding anybody else's gods, for in the Book of Exodus, we are told plainly, 'I am the Lord thy God, which have brought thee out of the land of Egypt, out of the house of bondage. Thou shalt have no other gods before me.' Which sounds very clear and to the point.

Not only must Christians and Jews have no other gods, they are to adopt a pretty hard approach to anybody who serves other gods or even does things like telling fortunes. The Book of Leviticus and the Book of Deuteronomy, both of which are part of Christian scripture, are uncompromising about wizards and witches,

> Do not turn to mediums or necromancers; do not seek them out, and so make yourselves unclean by them: I am the Lord your God. (Lev. 19:31)

> If a person turns to mediums and necromancers, whoring after them, I will set my face against that person and will cut him off from among his people. (Lev. 20:6)

> There shall not be found among you anyone who burns his son or his daughter as an offering, anyone who practices divination or tells fortunes or interprets omens, or a sorcerer or a charmer or a medium or a necromancer or one who inquires of the dead, for whoever does these things is an abomination to the Lord. (Deut. 18:10-13)

And of course, perhaps most damning of all, Exodus 22:18 gives the stern injunction that, 'Thou shalt not suffer a witch to live'.

When even telling somebody's fortune or interpreting omens are looked upon as acts of wickedness, it is not hard to see that there would be what we might call today a clash of cultures when Christianity reached those parts of Europe ruled by the Roman Empire. Foretelling, or attempting to foretell, the future and the other practices forbidden in the Bible were so common at that time that they formed an almost unnoticeable backdrop to life in Europe. What could possibly be wrong with contacting the dead and using spells to blight crops or cause them to flourish? Actions of this kind were the proper business of wizards and priests and nobody thought anything more about it. A woman like Boudicca who divined the future by using a hare might have been a terrible annoyance to the Romans when she went to war with them, but her actions as a seer were nothing out of the ordinary to them. They and the Greeks had plenty of seers of their own doing much the same kind of thing.

To see that people who were in in effect witches and wizards were held in honour by both the Romans and Celts, one only need look at the story of one of the most famous witches in Europe, a woman called Veleda. Veleda, whose name derives from a root meaning 'seer', lived in a tower to which general access was not allowed. Only her acolytes were allowed to communicate with her and pass on her prophecies, predictions and advice to those who sought it. One is irresistibly reminded of the story of Rapunzel, who also lived in an inaccessible tower with a witch. It is fascinating to reflect on the idea of the witch in the tower who was attended by a young maiden. Was the Rapunzel in the fairy tale being trained as an acolyte? This might explain why she became useless to the witch once her virginity was lost. One remembers the Vestal Virgins of Rome, whose religious duties were bound up with their virginity.

Veleda was the chief seer of an area in modern-day Germany, which was at that time under Roman dominion. Around 70 AD, some of the tribes in what in that part of northern Europe rebelled against the rule of Rome. The leaders of the revolt came to Veleda's tower and asked what she foresaw. She told them that they would be successful if they attacked the Roman troops stationed nearby, which proved to be true. The garrison at Novaesium, which was at what is now the German town of Neuss, surrendered without fighting, as did the one at Castra Vetera. Ultimately though, the military power of Rome was too great for such a small local uprising to have any hope of success in the long term. What was surprising though was that even after they had regained control of the district, the Romans took no reprisals against the woman whose prophecy had been instrument in sparking the attacks on the Roman camps. The Romans believed that she had simply been doing her job and predicting the future. This was the kind of thing which they understood and respected, so even when they were victorious, the seer in her tower was left unmolested.

Attitudes towards witches like Veleda changed dramatically when Christianity was adopted as the official religion of the Roman Empire. None of this boded well for the wizards and witches of Europe. Since the arrival of the Yamnaya, perhaps 2,000 or 3,000 years before anybody in Europe heard about the Bible, the magicians and seers had been at the top of the social order, seen variously as priests and prophets, sometimes as leaders of the people, always revered and treated with the respect due to educated people who knew more about both the natural world and that which was unseen that either peasants or warriors. There are tantalizing glimpses in the Bible of the conflict which occurred when the first evangelists came into contact with the far older tradition of Yamnaya shamanism.

A few years after Jesus was crucified, the Apostle Paul, who was sometimes known by his original name Saul, went to Cyprus with a companion to spread the word about Christianity. There were various wizards on the island who took this visit ill and opposed the new religion. When they reached Paphos, the two missionaries were summoned to see the local Roman governor, who was intrigued by what he had heard about Jesus. The Bible tells us what happened next.

> The governor called Barnabas and Saul before him because he wanted to hear the word of God. But they were opposed by the magician Elymas (that is his name in Greek), who tried to turn the governor away from the faith. Then Saul – also known as Paul – was filled with the Holy Spirit; he looked straight at the magician and said, 'You son of the Devil! You are the enemy of everything that is good. You are full of all kinds of evil tricks, and you always keep trying to turn the Lord's truths into lies! The Lord's hand will come down on you now; you will be blind and will not see the light of day for a time'. (Acts 13:8-12)

The 'magician' was duly blinded for a few days and, according to scripture, the governor was promptly converted to Christianity.

Two things strike us about the above passage. The first is that the man whom Barnabas and Paul meet in Paphos is clearly a seer and wizard of some description. The second is that Paul does not hesitate to identify him with the Devil of Judaism and Christianity; he feels that the Devil of his own religion must be urging this 'magician' on against the spread of Christianity. Since on Cyprus, as in Greece and other parts of Eastern Europe, the Horned God was a prominent figure, we see here a very early instance of the identification of the Horned God as being the Christian Devil under another name.

After leaving Cyprus, the two missionaries who were so intent on spreading the good news about Christianity took ship and sailed to what is now Turkey, but was then part of the Greek sphere of influence. They travelled to a city in Anatolia called Lystra, where Paul healed a cripple. It was then that they encountered a very old tradition, one which we have seen already; the idea that the gods might come down to earth and walk about in human form. The Book of Acts takes up the story and tells of the reaction of people to hearing Paul and Barnabas speak and particularly seeing the miracle performed on the man who had been unable to walk from birth.

> When the crowds saw what Paul had done, they started shouting in their own Lycaonian language, 'The gods have become like men and have come down to us!' They gave Barnabas the name Zeus, and Paul the name Hermes, because he was the chief speaker. The priest of the god Zeus, whose temple stood just outside the town, brought bulls and flowers to the gate, for he and the crowds wanted to offer sacrifices to the apostles. (Acts 14:8-13)

Here too, there are several interesting points to consider. There can be no doubt that for the Greeks living in this town, the idea that their gods would condescend to come down to earth and visit them was not a remarkable or far-fetched idea. Indeed, after seeing a miracle performed, it was the most likely explanation for what they had witnessed. Many men, on being mistaken for gods, might be a little flattered, even if they then explained that this was not the case, but the reaction of Paul and Barnabas was one of the utmost horror and detestation for the very idea of such a thing being considered possible,

> When Barnabas and Paul heard what they were about to do, they tore their clothes and ran into the middle of the crowd, shouting, 'Why are you doing this? We ourselves are only human beings like you!' (Acts 14:14)

The behaviour of Paul, the man responsible more than any other for the establishment of Christianity as we now know it in Europe, did not bode at all well for the existing religious and magical traditions in the areas where Christianity took hold. The Romans, Greeks and Celts might have been tolerant of differences in each other's beliefs, but that was because all sprang from a common root, that of the Yamnaya. This furious god who was so jealous that he could brook no competition was a different matter entirely. Where Christianity became the main religion, there was no room for any competition or compromise. Other people's beliefs were just plain wicked and if they did not mend their ways then they would end up being killed; it was as simple as that. Although it took centuries for Christianity to become powerful enough in Europe to mount crusades, witch trials and inquisitions to root out and destroy heterodox views, the seeds were there from the very beginning.

There was of course traditionally no clear dividing line in Europe between those whom we might regard today as priests and others whom we would have no hesitation in calling wizards or witches. With the rise of Christianity, the leaders of other religions were treated as being enemies of the one true god and those who purported to foretell the future, interpret dreams and anything else like that were regarded as doing the Devil's work. It was so simple and clear-cut for the Christians. If anybody prophesied, spoke about religion or expressed a view about morality, the acid test was whether they were speaking in Christ's name. If so, all well and good. If they did not acknowledge the validity and unequivocal truth of Christianity though, then they must inevitably be speaking on behalf of the Devil. It was in this way that the horned god Cernunnos, in all his incarnations and disguises came to be seen as identical with the Satan of Judeo-Christian tradition.

Before Christianity spread into Europe, neither Jews nor Christians had any idea what Satan actually looked like. He was vaguely believed to be a fallen angel and was widely thought of as cognate with Baal, the god of the Phoenicians. Statuettes of Baal usually show him as a winged human, often holding a thunderbolt. This of course tied in

How Christianity made Wizardry Disreputable 141

with the idea that he had once been an angel. With the discovery that a lot of people in Europe had a soft spot for a supposed god with some of the attributes of an ungulate, that is to say horns on his head and hooves for feet, everything became much clearer. In Europe, at least as far as Christians could see, Satan took the form of a man with horns and cloven hoofs. From then on, that is how the Devil would always be thought of and the old version with wings was quietly dropped.

From this, it followed naturally that anybody who was at all involved with calling upon any horned god for help in divination or perhaps success in agriculture and so on, the kind of thing which wizards and witches were up to from time to time, was obviously in league with the Devil. All this found its way into the law in various European countries, including Britain.

It is necessary to pause at this point and assess the situation relating to wizards and witches in Europe after the fall of the Roman Empire. It has been suggested by some writers that groups of people clung tenaciously to an old religion and resisted the arrival of Christianity, continuing to worship their old gods. This idea forms the basis for the modern pagan or neo-pagan movement. The evidence for this idea is sketchy and not especially convincing. While it is undeniably true that an awful lot of people clung to old superstitions and had a vague reverence for fairies and fear of witches, there is no reason to suppose that this was part of a systematic religion which was driven underground by the arrival of Christianity. If anybody was responsible for the survival of images such as the Horned God, it is more likely that it was the Christians themselves. It is true that as missionaries spread the faith across Europe they encountered tribes who worshipped different gods and that these included the one-eyed sorcerer and also the human figure with antlers or horns. It took only a few centuries to suppress these though. This was done, as we have seen throughout this book, by reducing the old gods to the status of devils, wizards and witches.

Paintings and carvings of the Horned God, together with the one-eyed god whom most of us know as Odin are certainly found in Europe up to the time that the Roman Empire officially adopted Christianity in the fourth century AD. After that though, except in the northernmost part of the continent, they appear only in Christian iconography. There though, they depict not the horned god Cernunnos, but rather Satan of the Bible. If people in the Middle Ages were aware of the human figure with horns on his head, then they would identify him with the Prince of Darkness, rather than with some lost god.

Much the same applies to wizards and witches. Such people certainly filled the role of priests and priestesses in Celtic Europe and even earlier, but by the time that the Roman Empire fell, they had lost this position and were more properly viewed as mediums who purported to foretell the future and also doctors prescribing herbal remedies. They would also cast spells and give advice on matters ranging from love affairs to agricultural difficulties. Nobody though saw them as part of a religion.

A number of religions flourished in Europe 2,000 years ago, but all had fallen into disuse within a few years of the triumph of Christianity, a religion which would brook no rivals. When a temple dedicated to the god Mithras was unearthed in London in the 1950s, the statuary from it was found buried nearby. Mithraism had gone the same way as the old religion of the Celts. At Southwark Cathedral in London, a well was uncovered which was found to contain various statues and other objects which were evidently sacred to a pre-Christian religion. They had presumably been thrown into the well to protect them from the iconoclasm of the Christians. These religions fell into obscurity with the rise of Christianity and there is no reason to suppose that the gods which were worshipped by the Celts fared any better.

For the Christian Church, anybody healing another without the aid, or at least acknowledgement, of Christ, was viewed in a very poor light. Any power possessed which did not come from the Lord of the Bible must, by definition, be from the Devil. As for predicting the future, this was utterly forbidden and the Bible prescribed death for such individuals. Necromancy, the summoning up of the dead, was especially frowned upon. The more puritanical kind of Christian has always disapproved of playing cards, partly because they are used for gambling but also because they have often been used for telling the future. Not for nothing was the Tarot deck known in some quarters as 'the Devil's picture book'!

In the modern world, this all sounds most peculiar. Most towns in Britain have at least one spiritualist church, where people go for the sole purpose of witnessing and, they hope, participating in the practice of necromancy. Dead relatives are routinely summoned up and their counsel sought. Private sittings with mediums are also common enough. The decline of organized religion and the end of Christianity as a major influence on the lives of most people in Europe has meant that wizards and witches, along with necromancers and fortune-tellers, are free to behave as they please. This is a fairly new development though. Within living memory, people in Britain were still being imprisoned under the witchcraft laws for contacting the dead.

In 1735 the law in Britain as it related to witchcraft was changed. The last witch executed in the British Isles was Janet Horne, an old woman who was burned alive in Scotland in 1727. Even at that time, this was something of an anachronism and it was felt to be high time that the law was changed. The general view of most educated people, including ministers of the Church, by the early eighteenth century was that there was really no such thing as witchcraft and that those who claimed to be able to cast spells or tell fortunes were either deluded fools or frauds.

The 1735 Witchcraft Act did away entirely with the crime of being a wizard or witch and instead made it an offence, punishable by a maximum of one year's imprisonment, to claim that any human being had magical powers or was able to practise witchcraft. There were very few prosecutions under the new Act, because those who wished to have their fortunes told or to be put in touch with their dead fathers and so on were happy to pay for the services of those who claimed to provide such things. In Scotland in 1805 Jean Maxwell, who was known as the Galloway sorceress, was convicted and locked up for a year, in addition to being put in the stocks. Generally though, the law ceased to interest itself with witches and wizards. The last two cases brought under the Act are of interest, because they both entailed trials at London's Old Bailey during the Second World War. One of these ended in the last imprisonment for anybody under the Witchcraft Act.

By the time of the Second World War, mediums and séances had become an amusing subject for most people. So many fraudulent mediums had been exposed that for the ordinary person there was something irresistibly comic about the idea of summoning up the dead. Necromancy, in which wizards and witches had engaged for thousands of years, was a joke. In 1941 a play by Noel Coward was staged in London. Called *Blithe Spirit*, it poked a little gentle fun at the idea of séances and spiritualism. Coward had been inspired by the stories circulating in newspapers about various mediums who had been exposed as cheats. One of these was a Scottish woman called Helen Duncan. During the 1930s Duncan had been revealed on several occasions to be tricking credulous dupes by producing 'ectoplasm' and conjuring up ghosts. She did this by swallowing quantities of egg white and cheesecloth and then vomiting them up in the gloom of a séance. In 1933 she had been convicted in Edinburgh of defrauding people of their money by such tricks and fined £10.

Helen Duncan continued to hire herself out as somebody able to contact the dead and cause them to materialize in front of grieving relatives, but when the war began in 1939 she started to exploit the families of soldiers and sailors who had died fighting and this drew the attention of the authorities once more to her activities. In particular, she claimed to have been told by the spirits that HMS *Barham*, a Royal Navy battleship, had been sunk in 1941. This was true, but the loss had not been publicized. As a result, the navy began to take an interest in Duncan's séances. In 1944, Helen Duncan overreached herself in no small measure. She materialized one of her cheesecloth figures at a séance and told one of the sitters that this was the spirit of his dead aunt. She followed this up by producing another ghost, telling the man that this was his sister. This was a false move for two reasons. In the first place, the man to whom she made these claims had neither a dead aunt nor a dead sister. Secondly, and disastrously for Duncan, the person upon whom she practiced this imposture was Lieutenant Worth of the Royal Navy and he was there specifically to see what Duncan was up to.

The fact that she had been extracting money from the grieving widows and parents of servicemen killed in action was viewed as being so reprehensible that the full weight of the law was brought down upon Helen Duncan. She was charged under Section 4 of the 1735 Witchcraft Act, which covered those pretending to contact the dead. Three other people were charged with her, including her agent. The authorities were determined to make an example of Helen Duncan and in April 1944 she appeared at the Old Bailey. The judge refused to allow her to demonstrate her abilities by conducting a séance in the court and after she was found guilty, he sent her to prison for nine months.

Winston Churchill was very irritated to see the Old Bailey wasting its time on what he called the 'obsolete tomfoolery' of a trial featuring the Witchcraft Act and although there was to be another conviction for a similar offence in September that same year, it was obvious to most sensible people that it was time to do away entirely with legislation relating to witchcraft. In 1951, the Act was repealed and replaced with the Fraudulent Mediums Act.

The overall effect of Christianity on the way in which people view wizards and witches has been entirely negative. Either they are seen as wicked people in league with the Devil or, failing that, as unscrupulous charlatans, whose chief interest is in parting the gullible from their money. The idea that anybody could genuinely believe in such things as prophecy, necromancy and healing by supernatural means has never even been considered by either lawmakers or priests in Europe. This attitude to witches has had a very bad effect and led to the persecution and even murder of those suspected of practising magic. Such things, just like imprisonment under the Witchcraft Act, have happened within living memory. Sometimes, such deaths look very similar to the ritual killings whose victims turn up today as 'bog bodies'. The most recent case of such a killing of a supposed wizard took place the year after Helen Duncan was jailed. It was a curious affair and to set it in context we shall devote the next chapter to studying similar cases which took place in the eighteenth and nineteenth centuries. There are similarities between the English cases at which we shall be looking and the death of Bridget Cleary, which we examined in Chapter 10.

Chapter 12

Ritual Sacrifice in Modern Britain

In this chapter we shall be looking at the way in which some of the very old practices and customs which we examined lingered on into the nineteenth and twentieth centuries. We are talking here not of the nonsensical modern witchcraft movement, dreamed up by people like Margaret Murray, Gerald Gardner and Aleister Crowley, but rather the authentic traditions which were somehow overlooked by the Enlightenment and the Industrial Revolution, managing to cling on in out-of-the-way corners of rural Britain. Modern versions of magic, such as Wicca, are carefully manufactured confections which have no connection with the real world of the wizards and witches at which we have been looking in this book.

The phrase 'modern age', used in the title of this chapter, is perhaps a misnomer. We shall be looking only at events from the eighteenth, nineteenth and twentieth centuries. The focus will be upon the practice of ritual human sacrifice, the last known case in Britain of this being as late as 1945.

When we looked at the circumstances surrounding the deaths of the so-called 'bog bodies', it was noted that these people did not appear to have died in the course of a robbery or as a result of ordinary judicial execution. Instead, they were killed in circumstances which suggest strongly that there was a religious or sacrificial element to their deaths and that this was the ultimate reason for their being killed. In particular, it was noted that these victims were deposited in watery places and that this seemed to be an essential part of the ritual surrounding their killing and the subsequent disposal of their bodies.

Apart from the peculiar method of the deaths inflicted on the bodies recovered from bogs in Britain and Europe, there was also the possibility that these were not ordinary people, but rather those belonging to a special class; perhaps the nobility, even royalty or religious leaders. It has been suggested that the druids even sacrificed their own, because they were often the most important people in the land. A wizard's death would have been a powerful act of magic indeed, if conducted in the proper way, with the correct rituals and culminating in a threefold death.

The eighteenth century saw the last instance of anybody being sentenced to death in England for witchcraft, although thankfully the conviction was set aside and the sentence never carried out. Jane Wenham was an old woman living in Hertfordshire and in 1711 she was widely rumoured to be practising witchcraft against her neighbours, by means of casting spells. She was a spirited woman and took legal action for defamation of character against a farmer who had been spreading stories about her supposed magical abilities. Although she won the case, the damages awarded were paltry, amounting to just a shilling or 5p in modern currency.

Understandably disappointed to see that her good name was valued at such a trifling sum, Jane Wenham was heard by bystanders to mutter angrily that she would have justice in 'some other way'. This casual remark was interpreted by many people to mean that she would resort to magic to have her revenge. One of those involved in deciding the amount of damages which she should be awarded was a local vicar and when his maidservant fell ill, it was popularly supposed that she was bewitched. Jane Wenham was arrested and charged under the Witchcraft Acts, which at that time allowed the death penalty to be imposed. Indeed, hanging was mandatory for those found guilty of this offence.

On 4 March 1712, Jane Wenham appeared before Sir John Powell at the Assizes, which were roughly equivalent to today's Crown Court. Powell, who was a Member of Parliament as well as a judge, made no secret at all of the fact that he found the proceedings absurd, as the following exchange will show.

There were sixteen witnesses for the prosecution, including three clergymen. The judge, who was a witty, urbane and sophisticated man with no time for anything which smacked to him of the irrational, listened in undisguised amazement at the evidence which was presented to the court. The Reverend Strutt, for instance, testified that he had tried to check if the accused woman really was a witch by getting her to recite the Lord's Prayer. She kept stumbling though over, 'lead us not into temptation and deliver us from evil'. At first, she said, 'lead us not into no temptation and evil' and then, shockingly, 'lead us into temptation and evil'. For him, this seemed to clinch the matter.

One farm labourer gave evidence that he had seen the old woman flying, whereupon Powell addressed Jane Wenham directly, saying, 'You may fly. There is no law against flying.' Despite this and similar interruptions in which the judge made his own feelings very plain, the jury brought in a verdict of guilty and John Powell was compelled to sentence the woman to death. He refused to specify a date for the execution though and as soon as the trial was over, he used his influence to obtain a royal pardon for Wenham, who was then released.

Passing mention has been made of the last lynching of a suspected witch in Britain by a mob. In the summer of 1751 a handwritten notice began circulating in the Hertfordshire town of Tring, which alleged that a witch was living among them and would be drowned on a certain date. It read,

> This is to give notice that on Munday next there is to be at Long Marcon in the parish of Tring two ill desposed persons to be ducked by the neighbours consent.

Although 'ducking', that is to say submerging a woman convicted of minor offences such as being a scold, was a legal punishment, this was another matter entirely and anybody reading this message would understand that something more serious was being talked of. It must be remembered that it was less than 40 years since the last death sentence had been passed for witchcraft in England and that the fear of witches was still a very real one.

On the day specified in the pamphlet being passed from hand to hand in Tring, a large and angry mob assembled. The target of their fury was an old woman called Ruth Osborn and her husband John. The incident which had led to what was about to become a lynching was that Ruth Osborn was in the habit of begging from door to door at the farms surrounding Tring. After she had been turned away from one farm, she was seen to be muttering angrily and some of the calves on the farm later fell sick. This led to a rumour that Ruth Osborn had bewitched them.

The Osborns were staying at the local workhouse, but the man in charge was so worried for their safety that he took them to the nearby church, hoping that nobody would dare molest them there. When the crowd of people intent on mischief arrived at the workhouse, they demanded that the Osborns be turned over to them. John Tomkins, the master of the workhouse, refused and the men began smashing the windows of the building and demolished one end of it. Then they threatened to burn the place down and throw John Tomkins into the fire unless he told them the whereabouts of Ruth and John Osborn. Fearing for his own life, he told them what they wanted to know.

Showing scant respect for a place of worship, the mob dragged the Osborns from the church and stripped them naked. Then they tied their thumbs to their big toes and threw them in a nearby pond. Ruth Osborn struggled to the surface of the water, but she was struck with sticks and pushed back under until she drowned. Her husband survived, but only just.

The idea of placing witches or wizards in water in this way later acquired Christian overtones and was represented as a way of deciding their innocence or guilt, but the practice long predates Christianity. Those who drowned Ruth Osborn had already decided her guilt; they had every intention of seeing that she died in a horrible fashion, by being both drowned and also beaten. This reminds us of the fate of some of the bog people, who were both struck with blunt instruments and also garrotted, drowned and had their throats cut. Those who beat Ruth Osborn to death while simultaneously drowning her were following an older tradition for warding off ill fortune than they were perhaps themselves aware of.

Still, it may be objected, 1751 was long ago. Surely by the time that the Industrial Revolution was over and Queen Victoria had been on the throne for a quarter of a century, such behaviour would have become a thing of the past? We turn now to the Hedingham witchcraft case which took place in Essex in 1863. It may have been Victorian England at the height of empire, but the details of the crime sound as though the affair might just as easily belong in the Middle Ages. The edition of the *Bury and Norwich Post*, a local newspaper, for 15 March 1864, describes the victim of this killing thus:

> Dummy, who was deaf and dumb and about 80 years of age, had lived in a small mud hut near Sible Hedingham for the last 8 years and had been known in the neighbourhood for about 20 years, but his name and place of birth or his country were never known although he was generally supposed to be a Frenchman. His habits were peculiar and his inability to express himself otherwise than by grotesque gestures and was also very excitable caused him to be regarded by many as possessed of the power of witchcraft.

The man whose nickname was Dummy used to make a living of sorts by telling fortunes and advising young lovers of the probable outcome of their romantic longings. How he conducted such a business while apparently being wholly unable to speak is a curious point which none of the newspapers of the time explain. Although based at the village of Hedingham, Dummy used to walk out to other parts of the neighbourhood to offer his services as a fortune-teller or wizard. There was some doubt as to the exact nature of the old man's activities. On one of these trips, he found himself at a village called Ridgewell, where there was an alehouse run by a woman called Emma Smith and her husband. When evening came, Dummy wanted somewhere to sleep for the night and he indicated to Emma Smith that he would like to spend the night at her pub. When she refused, he began stroking the staff he carried in a strange way and somehow conveyed by gestures that he was very displeased.

From the day that she had refused the man known as Dummy a bed for the night, Emma Smith's health went into a decline. She became nervous and seemed to be wasting away. As the months passed, she persuaded herself that the nature of the problem was that she had been bewitched by the old man and that he alone could remove the spell he had cast upon her. Emma Smith accordingly travelled to Hedingham, sought out Dummy and begged him to come and stay the night at her alehouse, even offering him three sovereigns to do so. The man refused, drawing his fingers across his throat to indicate that he feared that she meant to murder him.

The exchanges between Emma Smith and Dummy took place in a public house called the Swan and there were many there who accepted that old Dummy was a wizard and that he might well have cast an enchantment on this woman. Feelings began to run high and when the Swan closed, a crowd followed Dummy out of the place. Emma Smith then tore off his coat and with the assistance of some of the crowd, hurled the old man into a stream. As she did so, she took Dummy's staff and began beating him with it. The result of this was that Dummy died a short while later of inflammation of the lungs, which doctors attributed to his being submerged in cold water. Emma Smith and a man who helped her were sent to prison for six months for assault. The affair became known as the Hedingham Witchcraft Case.

A few years later came the killing of another witch. Eighty-year-old Ann Tennant lived in the Warwickshire village of Long Campton. On the afternoon of 15 September 1875 she left her home to buy a loaf of bread. As she walked along the village street, a young man called James Heywood attacked her with a pitchfork, stabbing her repeatedly in the legs and body. He ended by thrusting the pitchfork through Ann Tennant's head. After his arrest, Heywood told the police that he had killed the woman because she was a witch. At his trial, he did not deny that he had killed Ann Tennant, but claimed that he had done so to protect the village, because the dead woman had bewitched cattle and crops. He went on to say that, 'If you had known the number of people who lie in our churchyard, who, if it had not been for them would have been alive now, you would be surprised. Her was a proper witch.' Perhaps unsurprisingly, Heywood was found not guilty by reason of insanity and spent the rest of his life in Broadmoor.

In Scotland too, the belief in witches and wizards still existed and they were regarded by some of the less educated inhabitants in out-of-the-way places as being as real a hazard to farmers and fishermen as stormy weather. In 1878 a young man appeared in court in Dingwall, charged with assaulting an old woman. He was the owner of a fishing boat, which he claimed had been bewitched, so preventing him from catching anything. It was said locally that shedding the blood of the wizard or witch responsible for this would lift the spell. When he was sentenced to a term in prison, he remarked that, 'It is hard to think that I should be put in prison, for the Bible orders us to punish witches'.

The idea that the shedding of the blood of a wizard might bring prosperity or end a spell of bad harvests or fishing hauls is very likely the way of thinking which lies behind the bog bodies which are still being found. The themes common to both the deaths which they suffered and the attacks on supposed witches and wizards in the eighteenth and nineteenth centuries are a belief that a curse is causing harm or damaging somebody's livelihood and that the remedy lies in inflicting injuries upon or killing a wizard. The injuries are often a combination of beating or stabbing and drowning. Such treatment was meted out to those we now know as bog bodies and was also seen when an old man or woman, thought to be a wizard or witch, was beaten and drowned in Britain 2,000 years later. Some very old tradition is being enacted in both cases.

The same year that Ann Tennant was murdered in Warwickshire, a baby was born in a village not far from Long Campden who was related to her. It was later suggested that she was the child's great-grandmother. The baby's name was Charles Walton and he too grew up to be popularly supposed a witch or, more accurately, a wizard. The fact is that there was a suspicion after her death that Ann Tennant had indeed belonged to a coven and that there was a tradition of witchcraft being practised in that corner of England. Be that as it may, Charles Walton grew up at Lower Quinton, which is only 15 miles or so from Lower Campden. As he grew up, Walton acquired a reputation for being able to tame horses and dogs by the power of his voice alone and it was said that birds flocked to him if he called them. He bred toads too, keeping them as pets, or as some said familiars, in his garden. There were rumours that he was part of a circle of witches in the area.

In February 1945, as the Second World War was drawing to a close, Charles Walton was 74 and, his wife having died some years earlier, he lived with his niece. Although old, he was hale and hearty and hired himself out as a farmhand. That month he was cutting back hedges for a local farmer. On the morning of 14 February, Charles Walton took his tools to work in a field on the slopes of Meon Hill, just outside the village. He was carrying no money and other than his tools had with him only a slice of fruitcake for his lunch. He also carried an old-fashioned pocket watch.

It is curious to note how various threads of old legends which we have touched upon so far should come together so neatly, because Meon Hill, where Charles Walton was working that morning, had long been associated with one of the ideas at which we looked in some detail in Chapter 7. Meon Hill was supposedly one of those places where the Wild Hunt took place. Arawn was the lord of the underworld in Welsh mythology and stories of his exploits seem to have spilled over into the

English Midlands. On certain nights, it was said that Arawn and his fellow hunters would lead a pack of fearsome phantom hounds on a mad ride around the summit of Meon Hill, seeking souls to carry off to the underworld.

On the morning of St Valentine's Day Charles Walton was hard at work in a field on one of the slopes leading up to Meon Hill. He had with him a pitchfork and a tool known as a trouncing hook. This was something like a short, ferociously sharp sickle. When Walton's niece returned home from her own work at six o'clock that evening, she was surprised and a little alarmed to find that her uncle was not there. She went to see a neighbour and the two of them went off in search of Charles Walton. They found him where he had been working that day.

The sight which met the two people in the field that day was unbelievably horrible and bore a distinct resemblance to some of the human sacrifices at which we have previously looked. Charles Walton walked with a stick and this had been used to beat him around the head and shoulders. His throat had then been cut with his own trouncing hook. The body of the old man had also been pinned to the ground with the pitchfork, which was driven through his neck. A curious circumstance was that his shirt had been unbuttoned and his trousers too unfastened. When the police searched the body, they determined that the pocket watch was missing, but it was not worth a great deal, being made of nickel. The theft of a cheap watch could hardly provide a sufficient motive for such a dreadful murder. The local police were swift to realize that they were quite out of their depth with a case of this kind and called on the assistance of Scotland Yard, who sent Chief Inspector Robert Fabian investigate.

It did not take 'Fabian of the Yard', as he was popularly known, long to realize that a very close-knit community was not going to cooperate with police officers from outside the area. Despite the most exhaustive enquiries, he was wholly unable to establish any motive or find a single person who might have benefited from Charles Walton's death. There were rumours locally that Walton was a wizard and he had a reputation for being able to foresee the future, but nobody expressed any animosity toward him. One thing which Fabian did learn was that the missing pocket watch might perhaps have some significance beyond its financial value. The details which were circulated to pawnbrokers and jewellers were certainly unremarkable enough,

> Gents plain white metal pocket watch, snap case at back, white enamel face, with "Edgar Jones, Stratford on Avon" thereon. Second hand. English numerals. Valued at 25/- about ten years ago.

Those familiar with old-style watches of this kind will know that they usually have a hinged cover protecting the glass of the face. Walton kept in this watch a round piece of black glass. It was described variously as a piece of 'witch glass' and also a 'scrying mirror'. Both these terms are archaic and indicate something similar in function to a crystal ball, allowing the owner to peer into it and foretell the future. It seemed bizarre, but could the desire to obtain this object this provide a motive for the murder of the old man? Even so, it would hardly have been necessary to carry out such a brutal slaying. There were far easier and less gory methods of disposing of a man who was 74 years of age.

Despite the most rigorous efforts, the police officer from London was not able to find anything which could lead to the killer. In his own mind, Fabian was convinced that the murder was related in some way to witchcraft, but that was only his suspicion; there was very little evidence upon which to base such a theory. No arrests were ever made in connection with the case. Most of the people in Lower Quinton seemed more interested in the fact that the previous year's harvest had been a particularly poor one, a concern which Chief Inspector Fabian thought odd, considering the awful crime which had taken place in the village.

Looked at objectively, the death of Charles Walton seems uncannily similar to the types of death inflicted on the bodies of victims from the Iron Age which have been retrieved from bogs in Europe. Two methods were used to kill him, both beating around the head so hard that his walking stick was covered in blood and hanks of hair and also his throat being slashed open. So violent was the assault upon him that several of his ribs were broken. Lindow Man also had a broken rib, as well as a cut throat. The fact that Walton had been pinned to the ground with a pitchfork was also strange and had a connection going back thousands of years to the methods used to deal with witches, wizards and those who might rise from the dead to torment the living.

We have looked at the subject of what are known as 'bog bodies', many of which date back to the Iron Age. There is one very curious feature about a number of these bodies which is worth noting and may provide us with a direct link through the ages and cast light on the murder of Charles Walton.

One of the so-called bog bodies from Denmark was found in 1835 and nicknamed 'Haraldskær Woman', due to the name of the estate where she was found. Not only had she been strangled and placed in a bog, about 500 BC, but she had been pinned down with wooden poles, as though to ensure that she could not rise up again. This had been done in a methodical fashion, with crooks placed over her knees and elbows, which had been hammered hard into the peat. It is unknown whether or not this woman was alive or dead when she was placed in her watery grave. A few years after she was discovered, a Danish magazine which was a little like the modern *Reader's Digest* was published. It was called *Light Reading for the Danish Public*. The edition of Friday, 8 March 1839 carried a piece about the 'Haraldskær Woman'. It read as follows:

> Every countryman will immediately recognize in this corpse the body of someone who when living was regarded as a witch and whom it was intended to prevent walking again after death. Many of us have either ourselves seen, or have heard old people speak of, stakes standing here and there which have been driven in in earlier times, since men first recognized the existence of

such restless spirits, by those who, having read of these matters in magical books, thought that by this means they could get the better of the ghosts. Our forefathers believed that so long as the stakes stood the ghost remained pinned in the ground.

This passage makes it clear that there was an association in the minds of those who found some of the bog bodies in Denmark between the circumstances of their deaths and the way that their bodies were disposed of, and the idea that they were wizards or witches. Just in case anybody should be feeling that those 'countrymen' mentioned in the article must have lived in remote backwaters with strange old customs to be aware of such things as driving stakes through witches, it is worth recalling that this kind of thing was common practice in London as late as the nineteenth century. Indeed, it was mandated by law until a few years before Queen Victoria ascended the throne.

That corpses were having stakes driven through them, so that they would not roam the earth after burial, was a very old tradition in Britain and doubtless had the same origins as those in Denmark; that is to say that it was something which had been going on for at least 2,000 or 3,000 years. Londoners in the eighteenth and nineteenth century added another means of confusing any ghosts, by not only driving stakes through the corpses but burying them at crossroads, so that if by some miscalculation they did rise from the dead, they would be puzzled about which way to go! Here is an extract from a newspaper report on the burial of a man called John Duke, who murdered his wife in 1761 and then killed himself by cutting his own throat.

> Wednesday night the body of John Duke the bricklayer, who lately murdered his wife in Thomas Street, Drury Lane, and afterwards cut his own throat, and died in the hospital, was buried in the Cross-Road near St. Giles's Pound, with a stake drove thro' his body, the Coroner's Inquest having brought in their verdict, Felo de se.

'Felo de se' is the old expression for suicide and suicides were thought to be especially likely to haunt the earth after death. John Duke's body lies beneath the office block of Centrepoint.

This means of dealing with the bodies of suicides was still going strong well into the nineteenth century. In 1811 John Williams, the man suspected of some grisly crimes which became known as the Ratcliffe Highway Murders, managed to hang himself in his prison cell where he was awaiting trial. On the night of Monday, 30 December 1811, Williams' body was set on a cart and paraded through the streets of East London. It was then taken to the crossroads where Cannon Street Road and Cable Street intersect. Once it had been placed in the grave which had been dug there, a stake was hammered through the dead man's heart, pinning him in his grave.

By the time of John Williams' strange burial, the Industrial Revolution was in full swing and it must have been apparent to any educated person that this bizarre practice had no place in the modern world. It continued though for another 22 years. In 1833 a young man called Abel Griffiths killed himself and was duly buried at a London crossroads at dead of night with a stake being hammered through the body. This took place at the site of what is now the bus station outside Victoria railway station and was to be the last such occasion. The law was changed that year, forbidding burials of this kind in the future.

It has been necessary to go into some detail about the use of stakes to prevent ghosts rising from the dead in Britain to show that this was a custom which was identical to that seen in European bodies from the Iron Age. That it lingered on until the age of the steam engine and factory just goes to show how popular ceremonies like this can be. The staking of a body at a crossroads always drew curious crowds to watch the awful proceedings.

Returning now to the murder of Charles Walton, we look at one final bog body and the precautions which had accompanied its burial. On 9 January 1952 the body of a man, dating as usual from the Iron Age according to all the evidence, was unearthed in the south of

Denmark, not far from the border with Germany. This man had also been fastened into his final resting place, but not with a stake through his body. Forked branches had been sharpened and hammered over and in places into this Iron Age victim. One branch was pressing his throat into the peat of the bog.

The methods used on both the bog bodies from 2,000 years and also more recently on those who killed themselves, are eerily reminiscent of what was done to Charles Walton after his throat had been cut. Was he pinned to the earth as a symbolic way of preventing his spirit from rising up to haunt the area or seek vengeance against his killer? We remember too when looking at this murder that the traditional way of dealing with vampires and the undead, is by slashing their throats and driving a stake through them.

The similarities between the death of that old man in a field in the English Midlands and the sacrificial victims pulled out of Danish and German bogs are too great to be dismissed as mere coincidence. The rumours of witchcraft, the cut throat, the other injuries, being pinned to the earth by a spike driven through his body; this was almost a carbon-copy of the injuries suffered by the people whose corpses were deposited in watery graves a century or two before the birth of Christ. This was almost certainly the sacrifice or murder of a man believed by those around him to be a wizard. The only thing we are never likely to know at this late stage is what this death was intended to achieve. Was it something to do with the previous year's poor harvest? Did somebody feel that Walton had cast the Evil Eye on the crops and deserved to die as a result? Or could it be that shedding the blood of a wizard in the springtime and letting it soak into the earth would have the effect of restoring the fertility of the fields, one explanation which has been advanced for the bog bodies?

There was a strange coda to Charles Walton's murder. There was no doubt at all that he was wearing his pocket watch when he went to work on the day of his death; he never left his cottage without it. Chief Inspector Fabian was very keen to track down the missing watch, because he thought that it was possible that the killer's fingerprints might be found on it. He even managed to persuade an officer of the Royal Engineers regiment at a nearby army base to send a couple of men with mine-detectors to sweep the area where Walton had been found, but it was all to no avail. Neither that nor the notices circulated to jewellers in the Midlands brought the watch to light.

In August 1960 an outhouse near the rented cottage where Walton and his niece had been living in 1945 was demolished. Within it was found the watch for which everybody had been searching 15 years earlier. The cottage and outhouse had both been thoroughly checked by the police after the murder and it was inconceivable that they would have missed this vital clue. Besides which, why would Charles Walton have hidden the watch of which he was so proud in an outhouse? The only possible conclusion was that the person who murdered him had, for reasons which are completely obscure, felt the need to return the watch to the nearest point to the owner's home that could be safely done. Inside the watch was the small fragment of glass which Walton had used as an aid to seeing into the future.

What can we say about these deaths of reputed witches and a wizard? There can be little doubt that there are echoes of the sacrificial victims who have been unearthed from Iron Age Europe. Apart from the assaults and deaths which were a consequence of people believing themselves to be under a curse or enchantment, the death of Charles Walton has features of a quite common type of human sacrifice; that of the person whose blood is shed and sprinkled on the land to ensure a fertile season. Fabian was a little taken aback to find that local people in the farming community appeared to be more worried about the previous year's meagre harvest than they were about a bloody murder, but this could be more readily understood if Walton's death was seen by some of those living in the district as being likely to ensure a better harvest in 1945. This, after all, might have been the reason that some of those whose bodies have been recovered from bogs were killed and laid in the waterlogged earth.

Thinking of stakes through the bodies of wizards or supposed wizards and others whom it is hoped to prevent from wandering abroad after their death reminds us of the legendary end of the wizard Merlin. The *Scotichronicon*, a fifteenth-century history which owes much to old Celtic myths, relates an interesting story about the strange death which Merlin suffered. He was attacked by a band of shepherds who were the subjects of a minor king who was not a fan of Merlin's. The men beat and stoned the aged wizard and when he ran from them, he fell over a cliff, landing on a sharp stake which went through his body. As if all this was not bad enough, he found that his head was under the water of a nearby stream and so he died from being beaten, impaled and drowned. We looked earlier at the so-called 'threefold death' which was inflicted upon some of the bog bodies and this is precisely what befell Merlin. Is this sheer coincidence or is it yet one more instance of a folk memory being grafted onto a well-known figure?

Just as we instinctively encourage our small children to put out carrots on Christmas Eve for Father Christmas's reindeer or toss coins into wells, so too has the custom of beating and drowning particular people who may have magical powers persisted almost to the modern world. Had we asked any those people who plunged suspected wizards and witches into the water after first beating them just why they had done something so cruel, they would have been quite unable to answer. It is just what we do from time to time, especially if things are going wrong. The cases at which we have just looked, which took place in the eighteenth and nineteenth centuries, all followed people falling ill or crops failing. In ancient times, misfortunes of this kind might have been dealt with by inflicting a triple death on somebody of noble birth or perhaps upon a shaman. We have to work though with what we have and if a village only has a strange old man who keeps toads as pets or a woman who threatens to put the Evil Eye upon her neighbours, then these are the ones who will be chosen.

All these customs are part of our common cultural inheritance, even if we have not thought of it in such terms before. It forms part of a mental background through which we interpret the world. Despite the technological advances of the last century or two, the same traditions and rituals are still practised and taught to our children. How many readers have been involved in the strange ceremony of exchanging part of their body for wealth? Everybody who has ever left a tooth under their pillow in childhood and woken in the morning to find coins have been left by the fairies in exchange for it will know what we are talking about here!

Chapter 13

Our Cultural Heritage

The topics at which we have looked in this book are not merely some curious and obscure byway of European history, of little interest to anybody other than those with a fascination for folklore and superstition. The images and mythic archetypes which were current in the Neolithic and Bronze Ages are still of enormous importance today. Indeed, it might be said that they have shaped our world. Precisely because they are so pervasive, we hardly even notice the effect which subconscious memories of what I have described as the 'Magical Realm' have upon our lives. Everything from the architecture of London's major buildings to tastes in both popular books and what is sometimes known as high culture are permeated by the ideas at which we have looked in this book.

Let us begin with two seemingly very different aspects of our lives in the west, Disney films and the British Houses of Parliament. Underpinning both establishments is a vision of the past which calls to the deepest part of our psyche. The opening graphic sequence of films released by the Walt Disney studio shows a castle which might be the one in which Sleeping Beauty slumbered for a hundred years. It is instantly recognizable as being a fairy-tale vision of what a castle ought to look like. The castle is symbolic of the early films produced by the studio, such as *Sleeping Beauty*, *Snow White* and so on. It ties in too with the home of the beast in the more recent film, *Beauty and the Beast.* These films are of course based upon stories from the Bronze Age and the castle at the beginning of Disney films references these fairy tales in their later versions, those first written down at the time of the Tudors. We take all this for granted when watching the latest release from the Disney studios, but have readers ever asked themselves why the Houses of Parliament are designed to look like a fairy-tale castle as well, with all manner of strange little flourishes and unnecessary turrets? Why are the windows of Big Ben are tricked out to look like the slits in a castle wall from which archers might shoot in safety at a besieging force? The answer to this question lies also in the Bronze Age.

Although ostensibly set in the medieval world, the story of King Arthur has its roots long before that period. The traditional view today is that King Arthur was a Romano-British chieftain fighting against the invading Saxons. The motifs within the narrative though date from a much earlier period than the Dark Age which followed the Roman withdrawal from Britain in the fifth century AD. An overarching plot is the search for a magic cauldron, one of the central characters is a powerful wizard and we see incidents such as a prized sword being sacrificed in a lake. These ideas are from a much earlier era.

For thousands of years stories of, and images from, the magical realm were passed down by word of mouth. From time to time, some found their way into decorations on cauldrons or warriors' helmets. Sometimes, as in the case of Shakespeare's plays, some fragment of folk history which had perhaps been circulating for millennia was written down and thus survived to modern times. Herne the Hunter, leader of the Wild Hunt, is an example of this process. Sometimes, a concerted effort is made to set down in print odd pieces of ancient stories and legends which might otherwise have been lost. The Brothers Grimm did this with some fairy tales which later turned out to be very much older than anybody could have guessed. It was not until the nineteenth century that our ideas about the magical landscape in which Merlin the wizard lived, which served also as the backdrop to many fairy tales, was established in its present form.

At any rate, the story of Arthur and Merlin, as related in Thomas Mallory's *Le Morte d'Arthur*, had a very great influence upon Britain in later years. Four hundred years after this knightly fantasy of magical adventures, in what could pass for Tolkien's Middle Earth, became popular, it enjoyed a vogue with the Victorians. By the time that Queen Victoria had been on the throne for a few years, the novelty of the Industrial Revolution was beginning to wear off a bit and many middle and upper-class people began yearning for the forgotten glories of a distant past. Their dissatisfaction with the present took the form of a longing for the days of the magical realm where anything might happen through the agency of wizards and fairies, rather than the dull materialism of their own era.

The whole wizards, witches and fairies thing really took off in nineteenth-century Britain. Until that time, wizards and warlocks had been widely seen as sinister and often malevolent. It was only a century or two, after all, since men and women had been sentenced to death in England and Scotland for witchcraft. The wizard Merlin though, a central figure in the Arthurian myths, was portrayed as a benevolent old chap, like some kindly Victorian grandfather, concerned only with ensuring that the rightful heir ascended the throne of England. This simplified, some would say bowdlerized, version of the man of magic began the process of rehabilitation for wizards which has lasted to this day and is manifested in the popularity of the Harry Potter books.

This longing for a vanished and half-imagined past, based upon the folk memories at which we have been looking, permeated every aspect of Victorian life. The very streets were transformed by it; an effect which may be seen in modern London. Have readers ever stopped to ask themselves why such iconic buildings as St Pancras railway station are built like castles from the supposed age of King Arthur? Or for that matter, why the Royal Courts of Justice in the Strand, which often features in news photographs, is designed in the same style, as are the Houses of Parliament? The answer is very simple. Many of the most famous buildings from Victorian times are built in a style known as Neo-Gothic. The reason for this was to make town halls, railway stations and even the Houses of Parliament look as though they might have been there since the imaginary time of King Arthur.

While public buildings were being erected in a style which harked back to a lost time, rooted in our ideas of an heroic age of wizards and heroes, fairies and cauldrons, there were other developments. Art and literature were joining in this false nostalgia with equal enthusiasm. Alfred Lord Tennyson, the Poet Laureate, produced his cycle of epic poems called the *Idylls of the King*. These dealt with every aspect of the Arthurian myths and were hugely popular. In these and other poems, Tennyson wrote of the old idea of fairies as being enchantresses or witches of human size, rather than the dainty little creatures which others wished to see them as. Morgan le Fay, or Morgan the Fairy, was one of these, as was the Lady of Shallot, who featured in one of his best-known poems. In it, the eponymous character is referred to as, 'the fairy Lady of Shalott'.

Tennyson's poetry chimed with what was also happening in the world of fine art and also interior design. The Pre-Raphaelite Brotherhood, consisting initially of three British artists, were very keen on recreating Tennyson's fantasy version of the past in their paintings. William Holman Hunt, John Everett Millais and Dante Gabriel Rossetti were very taken with the idea of rejecting much of the modern world and retreating to a sanitised and visually appealing medieval landscape. Together with other artists they produced pictures showing the Lady of Shallot, the death of King Arthur and various other romantic scenes. While they were doing so, William Morris was busy producing designs for wallpaper and textiles as part of the Arts and Crafts Movement, which was also tied up with the rejection of the modern, industrialized and mercantile world of nineteenth-century Britain in favour of a past world. Queen Victoria and her husband were all in favour of this and Illustration 20 shows an extraordinary statue which may be found in London's National Portrait Gallery. It shows Queen Victoria and Prince Albert dressed as people from King Arthur's court at Camelot. The whole culture of this lost world of the romanticized past was so widely embraced that it came to sum up the era. Every time we look at a Victorian town hall built in that peculiar style, a pastiche of a castle like Camelot, we see just how deeply rooted the love of the past was.

Until the nineteenth century, most of the history and legends of the Indo-European societies which had flourished around 2000 BC were preserved only in the garbled stories which ordinary people, often in rural districts, had received from their parents and grandparents. Snippets of information such as iron being a good way to keep fairies at bay and the idea that witches could pose a danger to a farmer's livelihood if they put the Evil Eye upon his livestock or crops circulated by word of mouth. There were also garbled ideas relating to such things as King Arthur, mixed in with stories of the Wild Hunt and horned demigods like Herne the Hunter. Only when these began to be recorded in permanent form by folklorists like Joseph Jacobs in England and the Grimms in Germany did it become possible to form an overview of the landscape in which the earliest fairy tales took place and see that it closely resembled the legendary world of King Arthur.

This process of reviving and commemorating the Magical Realm was not of course limited to Britain in the nineteenth century and it reached its zenith in Germany. Richard Wagner revolutionized opera with his idea of the 'Gesamtkunstwerk', or total work of art. Music, drama and visual art were combined together to create a spectacle like nothing ever seen before. Wagner's major work, *The Ring of the Nibelung*, centred around old legends of dwarves, dragons and the pagan gods, including Odin. *Parsifal* was concerned with the quest for the magic cauldron which we call today the Holy Grail. That he chose legends with their origins in the Bronze Age for his greatest works was no coincidence. He believed that these tales epitomised the German soul.

We have already remarked that Wagner's stories of dwarves and magic rings take place in the same universe as *The Lord of the Rings*, but their influence runs far deeper than that. Nazi ideology, which led to both the Second World War and the Holocaust, was consciously modelled on the world which Wagner described – a pre-Christian age of paganism. The Third Reich was intimately associated with

Wagner, his music and his ideology and it is for this reason that it was until quite recently illegal to perform his music publicly in Israel. Not all the effects of the memories of the Magical Realm are desirable or good.

The twentieth century saw some of the great literary works set in the world at which we have looked. These were written for both adults and children and, as we remarked in the Introduction to this book, took place in similar kinds of location. Indeed, so similar are the worlds of books like *The Hobbit*, *The Chronicles of Narnia* and *The Sword in the Stone*, that one might almost say that they are a 'shared universe'. This idea, which is more commonly applied to comic books and films, suggests that various characters, even those imagined by different writers or producers, occupy the same, imaginary world. Perhaps a concrete example of this might make the concept a little more clear.

C.S. Lewis, author of *The Lion, the Witch and the Wardrobe*, was of course a friend of Tolkien, who wrote *The Lord of the Rings*. In the universe of Tolkien's books a large island called Numinor lay in the Atlantic Ocean, roughly where the legendary Atlantis was located. The same fate which befell Atlantis also caused Numinor to sink below the waves, an event described in detail in another of Tolkien's books, *The Silmarillion*. The name 'Numinor' was dreamed up by Tolkien and was supposed to have existed on earth thousands of years ago. In addition to *The Chronicles of Narnia*, C.S. Lewis write a trilogy of science fiction novels about interplanetary travel. In the concluding book, *That Hideous Strength*, the protagonist is talking to a resurrected Merlin. The conversation goes as follows,

> 'It may happen to seem to you the speech of barbarians,' said Ransom, 'for it is long since it has been heard. Not even in Numinor was it heard in the streets.'
>
> The stranger gave no start and his face remained as quiet as before, if it did not become quieter. But he spoke with a new interest.

'Your masters let you play with dangerous toys,' he said, 'Tell me slave, what is Numinor?'

'The true West,' said Ransom.

In the introduction to *That Hideous Strength*, Lewis has this to say about these casual references to Numinor,

> Those who would like to learn further about Numinor and the True West must (alas!) await the publication of much that still exists only in the MSS of my friend, Professor J.R.R. Tolkien.

It is clear then that although separated by some thousands of years, both *That Hideous Strength* and *The Lord of the Rings* are set in a universe where the island of Numinor once existed to the west of Europe. That C.S. Lewis's book centres around Merlin as well is also of note.

Readers might, for their own amusement, compile mentally a list of fanciful books, films, computer games or television series written, published, played, broadcast or shown in cinemas in the twentieth century which contained the following; a solitary wizard, a famous sword which is named, a wandering warrior who might be the heir to a throne, a lowly agricultural worker or artisan who has the ambition to become a warrior, or a race of smaller beings, human in outward appearance, who are treated with caution and a certain degree of suspicion. The list will, one imagines, be a fairly extensive one!

Because we are so familiar with these plot devices and characters we hardly stop to think about it when they crop up in a new film or computer game; seeing them, although we may not be consciously aware of the fact, as old and familiar friends in new guises. Take, for instance, the matter of a sword which has a particular name. Whether swords really were given heroic names in the distant past is an intriguing and debatable point, but in the universe of which we are talking, this is the commonest thing in the world. There can be few people who have not heard of King Arthur's sword Excalibur. In *Prince Caspian*, one of the books which C.S. Lewis wrote about the imaginary land of Narnia, one of the central characters says, 'It is my sword Rhindon, with it I killed the wolf'. Bilbo Baggins, the protagonist of *The Hobbit*, acquires a sword which he names Sting, after he uses it to evade some monstrous spiders. In *The Lord of the Rings*, the heir to the throne of Gondor has a very special sword which was formerly named Narsil, but had been reforged and given the name of Anduril; it is also known as the Flame of the West. Given all this, when people tuned into the television series called *A Game of Thrones*, they were already familiar with the convention of special swords being given names. One is called 'Oathkeeper', another 'Needle' and reference is made to another, centuries earlier, which had been named 'Dark Sister'.

We might say that the naming of special swords is by way of having been a tradition in heroic and fantastic literature for over a thousand years; we see it happening in the French epic poem *The Song of Roland*, which was written in the eleventh century AD. There is no history of such a thing in real life, apart from the occasional incident during the Crusades, which may well have been inspired by the highly romanticized events in *The Song of Roland*. That this practice is mentioned in old legends like that of King Arthur suggests that there existed a folk memory of its happening long before it was recorded in written form. The production of swords in the medieval world was an industrial process and the processes which contributed to the end product were fairly well regulated. There was a time though when the making of a sword was a highly individual activity and each one a special and precious artefact.

Like many of the things at which we have looked, the naming of swords as special and magical weapons probably began in the Bronze Age. At that time making a sword was a very different business from what it later became in the Middle Ages. The swordsmith in Bronze Age Europe had to cast each sword by heating up crucibles of molten copper and then mixing it with a carefully measured quantity of tin. The blade would then have to be hammered and shaped, an edge ground, and a handle fitted. Every one of those swords was an individual work of art, fit for a prince or, at the very least, a wealthy warrior. It would have been a little surprising if these precious blades had not ended up with a name to distinguish them from other swords.

This then is an instance of the cultural baggage which we have inherited from the distant past. It is so clearly delineated that when we watch a brand-new television series, we understand much of what is happening, or going to happen, because we have seen it all before in the books from our childhood. The special sword, the lonely wizard, the ambivalent attitude to the Little People; these are common threads with which we are all familiar. Let's look at a recent case of the way in which these mythic archetypes tap into our subconscious and strike a chord within us.

In 2018 a film was produced in the United States called *Aquaman*. It was based upon an American comic book hero whose adventures were first detailed as early as 1941, when he was fighting the Nazis during the Second World War. Aquaman's backstory changed a little over the years, but by the 1960s he was explained as being the product of an Atlantean mother who had married an American lighthouse keeper. They had named their son Arthur. From his mother, he inherited the ability to stay under water indefinitely and from his father a desire to protect the civilization on dry land from any attacks by forces from beneath the sea.

It is the film based upon these comic books which really brings into place the various themes at which we have looked in this book and shows that old myths like that of the king raised in exile, the quest for a magic weapon and so on are still very powerful influences upon the psyche of those raised in Europe and America. One need only mention that *Aquaman* became the second highest-grossing film ever produced by the Warner Brothers studio, coming in just behind one of the Harry Potter films. Professional film critics may have been a bit sniffy about it, but audiences voted with their feet and flocked to cinemas showing the film. What was it that made this such a huge success?

We have in this book several times mentioned the television series *Game of Thrones* and the fact that the eponymous hero of *Aquaman* was played by actor Jason Momoa, who was a key character in *Game of Thrones* probably helped to bring in the crowds. It was the story itself which the film told though which really attracted people. Arthur, the lighthouse keeper's son whose mother has vanished, is a king by birthright. He does not realize this as a child of course, because he is being raised in exile from the kingdom which he will one day rule. This is the theme of many old stories such as Theseus and of course King Arthur. The fact that Aquaman's given name is Arthur is hardly a coincidence. In childhood, Arthur is trained in special powers by a man who knows the boy's destiny and wishes to prepare him for the day when he claims his kingdom. In the film *Aquaman*, this role is undertaken by an adviser called Vulkor. Those familiar with the Walt Disney film *The Sword in the Stone*, loosely based upon the legend of King Arthur, will at once recognize Vulkor in the *Aquaman* film as playing a role analogous to Merlin the wizard.

Another element from Indo-European myth which is to be found in *Aquaman* is that of two brothers in mortal conflict. The story of Romulus fighting with and killing his own brother will spring to mind. Aquaman too has a brother, with whom he contends for control of the kingdom of Atlantis. Once again, this fraternal conflict featured in *Game of Thrones* and the struggle, ending in their deaths, between the characters known as 'the hound' and 'the mountain'.

It is intriguing to note that although *Aquaman* was only the second highest-grossing film produced by Warner Brothers, their top film also treats of broadly similar themes. In that film too we find that the protagonist is a boy who has a lofty destiny of which he is at first unaware. The Harry Potter films too are full of wizardry and also make reference to many of the ideas at which we have been looking. Lord Voldemort, to give one example, is seldom spoken of by name. There is very much a feeling of 'Speak of the Devil and he's sure to appear!'. Instead, people talk of 'You know who!' or 'He who must not be named'.

Some elements of these echoes from the past are of course more likely to strike a chord with us than others. Wizards and witches are one of these. The astounding success of the books about Harry Potter are a perfect illustration of this. We all grow up in the Western World knowing something about wizards and witches. Films like *The Wizard of Oz* tell us what witches look like and we receive a cultural top-up every year during the trick-or-treating which takes place on the night of the Celtic festival of Samhain, known to us these days as Halloween. The Harry Potter books tap into that knowledge with eerie precision. The deputy head of Hogwarts School is Minerva McGonagall and in the film, she is played by Maggie Smith. Needless to say, she wears a traditional witch's hat. Then there are magic wands, goblins and other motifs at which we have looked. The reason that these books and films appeal so widely in Britain is that they use the images which we all know.

We have seen in this book that wizards and witches are inextricably bound up with the history of the first Europeans and that the stories associated with them have as strong a grip upon us today as ever they did in the past. Every time we thrown a coin in a fountain, put out carrots for Father Christmas's reindeer or even find ourselves trying to make childcare arrangements for the half-term holiday, we will find that the shadow of the past still lays upon us and that activities and events which took place 5,000 years ago are shaping our lives even now in the twenty-first century. The history of wizards, witches and fairies, far from being an obscure and esoteric subject of interest only to the specialist researcher, permeate our everyday lives in a hundred different ways.

Appendix: The Magical Year

Ask anybody today how the year is divided up and they are likely to look at you as though you have asked a very silly question with an obvious answer. Everybody knows that the year is divided into twelve months and four seasons. What other way could there possibly be? As a matter of fact, the months and seasons are not nearly as significant in the lives of families, including older relatives who might be roped in for childminding or babysitting duties, as the system of seeing the year not as twelve or four parts, but rather eight. Looked at from this perspective and ignoring the way that we have, since the adoption of the Julian Calendar in 46 BC, counted the beginning of the year from 1 January, everything makes far more sense. After all, the selection of 1 January to start the year is wholly arbitrary, although after so many centuries it seems to us the natural way of ordering things.

Most people in Britain and many other parts of Europe do not talk in terms of months or seasons when planning for the year ahead. Instead, unwittingly, they divide the year into not twelve, but eight portions. For instance, In January we might say that we shall be going away with the children 'at half-term'. Or perhaps later in the year, we are look forward to Christmas or say that the children will be glad of the week off at half-term and that they always enjoy trick-or-treating at Halloween. That the spring half-term school holiday falls around the time of the Celtic festival of Imbolc or that the week off in autumn usually coincides with Samhain, is hardly noticed. Our year is, even today, divided up into a way which would have been quite familiar to Bronze Age Europeans. The names of festivals and celebrations have certainly changed, sometimes more than once in the last 5,000 years or so, but often the essential nature of the significant dates has remained unaltered.

The calendar which we use today is a relatively recent development and there is, as was remarked above, accordingly no particular significance attached to the first day of January, which we know today as New Year's Day. The old way of establishing points in the year which were important was based upon the solstices and equinoxes. In every year, regardless of which calendrical system one chooses to adopt, there will be a day when the hours of daylight last longest. This is the Summer Solstice, known in the modern world as Midsummer's Day. In the same way, there comes a point in winter when the opposite point is reached and daylight is at a minimum. Although this is sometimes referred to as Mid-winter, it is far more common now to celebrate a day which falls a little after the Winter Solstice and which we call Christmas.

In addition to the two solstices each year, there are also equinoxes, which are the days when the hours of daylight and those of darkness are equal. One equinox occurs in the spring and another in the autumn. So far, this natural process, looking only at the way in which the hours of daylight fluctuate throughout the year, has enabled us to divide each year into four parts. No calendar is necessary for this purpose. These quarters may then be subdivided once more, but this process requires the keeping of records or counting of days. Then we can work out a time of the year which is midway between solstice and equinox. In this way, the first European farmers hit upon the first important date following the Winter Solstice, which they called Imbolc. It falls midway between the Winter Solstice and the Spring Equinox.

Nobody knows for certain the derivation of the name Imbolc. A thousand years ago, it was suggested that it comes from the old pronunciation of words meaning 'ewe's milk'. It is sometimes pronounced as 'Oi-melk', rather than as it is written. Modern experts cast doubt upon this idea though, some suggesting that it comes from the Old Irish words relating to washing one's self. Whatever the truth of the matter, there can be no doubt that Imbolc has been celebrated since at least the Neolithic period or Late Stone Age. Some passage graves in Ireland, most notably the Mound of the Hostages, dating back 5,000 years, were constructed so that the light of the rising sun on Imbolc shone directly along a passage leading to the heart of the tomb.

Imbolc falls on 1 February in the modern calendar and is associated with lambing and the first signs of spring. It was the time of year when nature was stirring and divination by animals was used in an attempt to predict the weather likely in the coming year; a subject of great interest to an agricultural community. Using animals to foretell the future was not uncommon in the Celtic world and it is a practice which almost certainly predates their culture. It will be recollected that when Boudicca was about to lead an army against the Romans, she released a hare and interpreted the direction of its flight as a sign from the gods promising victory to her followers.

On Imbolc, wild animals would be observed and their behaviour used to predict the length of cold, winter weather remaining to be endured. An old proverb, first recorded in Scots Gaelic has it that,

> The serpent will come from the hole
> On the brown Day of Bríde,
> Though there should be three feet of snow
> On the flat surface of the ground.

The day of Imbolc was sacred to Bride or Brigid. The rule was that if the weather on Imbolc was sunny and bright, then winter was likely to linger on, but if it was cloudy and overcast, then spring would soon arrive. This old piece of divination is still practised in the United States, although perhaps in a tongue-in-cheek manner. Groundhog Day is on 2 February and if the shadow of the groundhogs, as they emerge from their nests, are visible, then this is a bad omen for the weather over the next month or two.

The way in which Christianity has appropriated the religious traditions of earlier cultures may be seen in the name now given to

Imbolc, which is St Brigid's Day. Originally, Brigid was a Gaelic goddess, cognate with the Celtic Brigantia or High One. Christian missionaries though invented a St Brigid and fitted her neatly into Imbolc. She is also sometimes known as Bride. This date is also Candlemas, which is also known as the Feast of the Purification of Mary. This refers to the ritual purification of a woman after childbirth. The Christian church has thus assured that it has two strong claims upon 2 February, ensuring that Imbolc is more likely to be forgotten.

Curiously enough, bearing in mind the Feast of the Purification, about this time of year the Roman festival of Lupercalia also fell. This too was a pastoral festival, marking the return of fertility after the winter. It was also known as 'dies Februatus', which means purification or purging. It is of course from here that the name of the month February is derived.

The next important time of year was the Spring Equinox, which comes on 21 March. The Christian festival of Easter is celebrated on the first Sunday after the full moon following the equinox. The association of rabbits with Easter, as in the Easter Bunny, has its root in the Celtic reverence for hares, which begin their mating rituals in March, at about the time of the Spring Equinox.

There is reason to believe that the Spring Equinox was once of much greater significance to the Indo-Europeans than it became after the Christians imposed their own festival of Easter, which fell at roughly the same time. One branch of the migrating Yamnaya headed west into Europe, but some moved south and east, ending up in India. Farsi, the language of Iran is Indo-European, for all that it is written today in the Arabic script. The Persian New Year is celebrated on the day of the Spring Equinox. This is not a festival recognized in Islam or Christianity, which suggests at a more ancient origin.

The real festival to follow Imbolc was of course Beltane and this coincides with what is known as Witches' Night in Germany. The celebration of Beltane, which takes place at the same time as May Day and also, in parts of Europe, Walpurgis Night, has its roots in the customs of the Yamnaya tribes, the Indo-European speaking peoples who spread out from what is now Ukraine, 5,000 or 6,000 years ago. We may be reasonably confident of this, because May Day has no relevance at all to the farming of crops. In other words, it was celebrated originally by pastoralists, those who kept or followed herds of livestock. Early May is when cattle are sent to their summer pastures, which means that this is almost certainly how May Day came to be a significant point in the year. We still mark May Day with a public holiday in Britain, despite the fact that it is thousands of years since we had anything to do with sending flocks to summer pastures.

The celebration of Beltane entailed lighting large bonfires. These, by means of sympathetic or imitative magic, would cause the sun to kindle and bring warmth to the earth over the summer. The cattle which were soon to be driven to the summer pastures were purified by being driven between two bonfires or sometimes urged to jump over the smouldering embers. This, it was felt, would strengthen or protect them.

Like Halloween, Beltane was a time when witches ruled and the Germans called the night before May Day, Walpurgis Night or, even more significantly, 'Hexenacht' or witches' night. The reason was simple. This was a time for celebration among the heathens of Europe before Christianity took hold. In Germany, Estonia, Finland and other Nordic countries, those following the old religious practices held the mid-point between the Spring Equinox and the Summer Solstice as being a special time. The bonfires which were lit were part of their way of encouraging the return of the warmer weather. This was anathema to Christians and a missionary called Walpurga managed to convert the German tribes and persuaded them to be baptised. Walpurga was an English woman, born in Devon in around 710 AD, who was determined to spread the faith as far as she could. She was very much opposed to the celebration of nature festivals and after she died, she was canonised on 1 May 870. This became another example of the way that Christians took over an old custom and put their own spin on it.

Instead of Beltane being the date when pagans and heathens got up to their old tricks, Walpurgis Night turned into a date in the calendar when everybody went to church and prayed for St Walpurga to protect them from witches. In the Czech Republic, the night of 30 April is known as Burning of the Witches. Effigies of witches are made and then thrown onto enormous bonfires, much as the British burn guys. In Estonia and Finland, this is the time of year for carnivals and fun.

There are clear and obvious parallels between Walpurgis Night and Halloween. In some rural parts of Germany it is accepted that young people will play practical jokes after dark, by rearranging things in people's gardens and sometimes daubing graffiti. One is reminded of the British and American custom of trick-or-treating, although without the soliciting of treats.

With the arrival of Christianity, the adherents of which religion frowned upon the pagan festival of Beltane, May Day became a substitute. Houses were decorated with green branches as a sign that the Earth had now come back to life again after winter. Dancing and other celebrations took place, many of them with a distinctly magical flavour. In fact some of the dancing around the Maypole became so obviously sexual and pagan in nature that the Church clamped down on it. Maypoles were burnt and celebrations banned. It is by no means impossible that the Maypoles are a relic of the very old European tradition of what have become known as 'pole gods'. These are crudely shaped wooden poles with human faces and often hugely exaggerated penises. The symbolism of young girls dancing around a tall wooden pole was felt by many respectable people in the sixteenth and seventeenth centuries to be unwholesome.

We come now to perhaps the most ancient point of all in the traditional calendar; one with a special association with fairies. This is of course the Summer Solstice, which we usually call Midsummer's Day. We know that there is a very long tradition in Britain of attaching special significance to this day because of course Stonehenge, which was constructed thousands of years before the birth of Jesus, was aligned so that the sun rises above what is known as the Heel Stone on the morning of Midsummer's Day. Like other festivals which have their origins with the Yamnaya, this day was marked by the lighting of bonfires, a custom which persisted in Scotland until the eighteenth century. It was once the practice for young men to leap as high as they could over these fires and the belief was that whoever jumped the highest, that would be the height to which the crops would grow that summer before they were harvested in the autumn.

The important point about Midsummer's Day was that it was the turning point of the year, the hinge if you like, when the days began to grow shorter and the slow march towards winter began. It was a time when the two worlds, the seen and unseen, collided and some invisible things came into sight. When Shakespeare called his play about fairies, *A Midsummer Night's Dream*, he did not simply pluck the title at random. This was the time of year above all others when one might catch a glimpse of fairies or even, if one was careless, even be carried off to their world. This was a similar idea to Halloween, only rather than ghosts and demons, it was the hidden people who were abroad.

Just as with other old beliefs, the Church was not overly keen on seeing people celebrating holy days which could not be connected, however tangentially, with Christianity. In this instance, they managed to turn Midsummer's Eve into St John's Eve, thus getting John the Baptist in on the act. This became woven into Midsummer's Eve in a curious way.

One of the customs associated with Midsummer's Eve in Britain was to hang bunches of a shrub known variously as goatweed or Demon Chaser around windows. This plant happens to blossom around Midsummer's day and so it was a nice way of brightening up the home with the yellow flowers. There was an old myth that anybody treading on flowering goatweed at that time of the year ran the risk of being carried away to the fairies' world. Hanging it up made the chances less of crushing it underfoot. Once the Christians began making sure that

John the Baptist was linked to Midsummer's Day, goatweed started to become known as St John's Wort. In recent years this has become a herbal alternative to taking anti-depressants prescribed by a doctor.

After Midsummer's Day came the great summer festival of Lugnasad, which was the beginning of the harvest time. We have seen that a successful harvest was of great importance to agricultural communities and to ensure that crops were plentiful and of good quality it was the practice to make sacrifices, including those of selected people. It need hardly be said that the Church was opposed to human sacrifice and so re-named Lugnasad as the Festival of the First Fruits, a time to give thanks to the Lord for the fertility of the ground. Villagers may well have attended Harvest Festival services at the local church, but in Britain until Victorian times they maintained their own rituals too. When the wheat was nearly all gathered in, a small stand was left in a corner of the field. This was the last refuge of the Harvest Spirit, a female deity. Since nobody wished to be the one to destroy her home, the workers would stop before the whole field was bare and take it in turns to throw their sickles at the remaining patch of stalks. When this had been done, they would gather up what remained and their wives would plait the stalks into a Corn Dolly or Kern Baby. This represented the mother goddess and was set in place of honour at the harvest meal which celebrated the gathering-in of the crops.

The old festival which we do still commemorate, and increasingly so in recent years, is of course the Celtic Samhain. This is roughly midway between the Autumn Equinox in late September and the Winter Solstice in December. Today, we know this as Halloween. If Midsummer's Eve is a time when fairies are sometimes visible to mortals, then Halloween is the opposite. It is when ghouls and evil spirits walk abroad and it is particularly associated with witches.

Samhain, pronounced Sow-wain, was another of those times of year when bonfires were lit. It is curious to note that in Britain, the bonfires have moved away from Halloween and are now popular more close to the midway point between equinox and solstice. The actual half-way between equinox and solstice is 7 November and of course on 5 November, bonfires are often seen, in celebration of Guy Fawkes' night. The fires were lit at this time of year as a symbolic way of prolonging the fading sun's heat and delaying the onset of winter. Like the other midway point between equinox and solstice, May Day, Samhain was marked by dressing up and disguise. Sometimes, young people would black their faces and engage in a version of trick-or-treating. Before pumpkins became popular, turnips were used to make jack-o'-lanterns. These were part of a myth which has more than a passing resemblance to the oldest known fairy tale in Europe, that of the smith and the Devil. In the jack-o'-lantern story, a notorious loose-liver and drunkard called Jack encounters the Devil while he is walking home one night from a drinking session. He manages to trick the Devil into climbing a tree and then carves crosses on the trunk to prevent his being able to climb down again. Jack strikes a deal with the Devil, that he will erase the crosses and release him, if the Devil promises that he will not allow Jack to enter hell. When Jack finally dies, he finds that he is not allowed into heaven because of all his bad behaviour during life. He goes down to hell, but true to his bargain, the Devil refuses him entry and, in irritation, throws a glowing coal at Jack's head. Because he is feeling a little cold, Jack hollows out a turnip and places the coal inside to preserve its heat. Then he sets off to look for a resting place, since neither heaven nor hell will have him. It is, allegedly, for this reason that we make jack-o'-lanterns at Halloween.

Halloween has always been a popular time of year to divine the future of course, a practice upon which the Church has always looked with disfavour, with strong scriptural backing. The fortune-telling at Halloween is of a fairly harmless nature. Girls can find out things about their future husband by peeling an apple in one continuous piece and then throwing it over their left shoulder. The peel will then form the initial letter of their future husband's name. Looking into a mirror in a darkened room on Halloween, lit only by a candle, it is said that an unmarried maiden will see the face of her future husband over her shoulder. If she should instead see a skull, then this is a sure premonition that she will die before she is married.

Halloween these days is marked by children dressing up as witches and ghosts, offering a mild threat to ordinary folk and exacting tribute from them. The sweets which we hand out to those knocking on our door on this night of the year are symbolic offerings to the dead, as represented by the small people masquerading as the spirits of the departed. Archaeological excavations at the sites of prehistoric burial places frequently find food which has been deposited in shafts dug near graves; the most practical way of offering food to those interred nearby. The modern, symbolic offering of sweetmeats to those acting the role of the dead is considerably more convenient.

The final festival of the year is one of the most ancient and long-lasting of them all. It is the Winter Solstice, when the sun might be about to fade away for good. Since early summer, the days have been growing imperceptibly shorter, until now the daylight is at its minimum. Each year, the unspoken dread was that the days would diminish further until the world was finally plunged into eternal darkness, a primeval and terrifying vision. This was the time of year, above all others, when the aid of the gods was needed to avert the ultimate catastrophe.

The Romans of course devoted themselves to a week of feasting at this time of year, known as the Saturnalia. In some ways, this was a precursor of the heavy drinking and gluttony which mark the modern celebrations which now centre around the Winter Solstice in Europe and America. For those people in ancient Germany, Britain and Scandinavia, the shortest day of the year was a time when the aid of the oldest and wisest of the gods was invoked. Odin, or his earlier avatars, arrived either seated on a horned beast or in a chariot drawn by a pair of animals with horns. He came in the middle of winter to reassure mortals that the sun would return to warm them and the days lengthen again.

Illustration 17 shows a later version of Odin as he was welcomed in the nineteenth century. He is wearing a hood, as was his custom when he came down to earth and mixed with ordinary people, and he is riding his cult animal, a large goat. This image is so clearly of a pagan god, that we might find it puzzling that anybody could ever have missed the resemblance to Odin, known in this guise as the Yule Father. The reason is very simple. Just as the early Christians commandeered some of the old gods and reduced them to the level of devils, so too they appropriated others and converted them to saints. Hence the Yule Father became transformed to St Nicholas. A corruption of this gives us Santa Claus, by which name Odin is generally known in the Western World.

The visits of Odin, as the Yule Father, had long been a feature of northern European folklore when the first Christian missionaries arrived. They encountered people who enjoyed feasting and celebrating at the time of the Winter Solstice and whose children looked forward to Odin paying the house a visit and giving them little presents. Nothing was easier for the Christians than to take over the feasting in the middle of winter and suggest that it should now be undertaken in celebration of the birth of their own god. The hooded and one-eyed god became St Nicholas and the Horned God, whose presence weaves in and out of all the oldest European legends, was rebranded as Krampus, a terrifying figure who was apt to carry off sinful children and then make them ritual sacrifices by the old method of drowning.

This then is the ancient cycle of celebration in Europe, one which has endured for many thousands of years. It was certainly well established by the time that megalithic monuments like Stonehenge were being constructed, as we can see by the way that they align to significant sunrises at key moments in the year. So familiar is this pattern that we seldom stop to ask ourselves *why* our year is ordered in such a way. We simply take it as read that the school holidays should fall on the Winter Solstice and the Spring Equinox, and that the longest holiday of all should be during the harvest-time. It has always been that way and that is that.

Not only is the rhythm of the year rooted deep in the religious observances of the Indo-Europeans, but also the months and days which we use reference pre-Christian history as well and their names date back thousands of years. We have examined Odin in considerable detail in this book and of course we remember him every Wednesday, which is Woden's Day. The months too are dedicated to the Roman gods of Janus, Mars, Juno and so on.

Bibliography

Ashe, Geoffrey (1990), *Mythology of the British Isles*, London: Methuen.
Ashe, Geoffrey (1968), *The Quest for Arthur's Britain*, London: Pall Mall Press.
Bahn, Paul G. (ed.) (1996), *Tombs, Graves and Mummies*, London: George Weidenfeld & Nicolson.
Brothwell, Don (1986), *The Bog Man and the Archaeology of People*, London: British Museum Publications.
Clayton, Antony (2008), *The Folklore of London*, London: Historical Publishing.
Cotterell, Arthur (ed.) (1980), *The Encyclopaedia of Ancient Civilizations*, London: The Rainbird Publishing Group.
Cotterell, Arthur and Storm, Rachel (1999), *The Encyclopaedia of World Mythology*, London: Anness Publishing.
Crossley-Holland, Kevin (1980), *The Penguin Book of Norse Myths*, London: Penguin Books.
Cunliffe, Barry *et al* (eds) (2001), *The Penguin Atlas of British and Irish History*, London: Penguin Books.
Frazer, J.G. (1890), *The Golden Bough: A Study in Magic and Religion*, London: Macmillan.
Glob, P.V. (1969), *The Bog People*, London: Faber & Faber.
Haywood, John (2008), *The Great Migrations*, London: Quercus.
Kightly, Charles (1982), *Folk Heroes of Britain*, London: Thames and Hudson.
Laing, Jennifer and Lloyd (1992), *Art of the Celts*, London: Thames and Hudson.
Mallory, J.P. (1989), *In Search of the Indo-Europeans*, London: Thames and Hudson.

Renfrew, Colin (1987), *Archaeology and Language: The Puzzle of Indo-European Origins*, London: Johnathon Cape.
Segal, Robert A. (2004), *Myth: A Very Short Introduction*, Oxford: Oxford University Press.
Sharkey, John (1975), *Celtic Mysteries: The Ancient Religion*, London: Thames and Hudson.
Spence, Lewis (1998), *Mysteries of Celtic Britain*, Bristol: Parragon.
Stevenson, Victor (1999), *The World of Words: An Illustrated History of Western Languages*, London: McDonald.
Webb, Simon (2011), *Unearthing London*, Stroud: The History Press.
Westwood, Jennifer (ed.) (1987), *The Atlas of Mysterious Places*, London: Marshall Editions.
Williams, Brenda (2006), *Ancient Britain*, Peterborough: Jarrold Publishing.
Wyse, Elizabeth *et al* (ed.) (1988), *Past Worlds: The Times Atlas of Archaeology*, London: Times Books
Zipes, Jack (ed.) (2014), *The Original Folk and Fairy Tales of the Brothers Grimm*, Princeton NJ: Princeton University Press.

Index

Abbots Bromley Dance 64
Actaeon 82–4
Andraste 96
Angel of Mons 78, 79
Anglesey 89, 91, 95, 98, 99
Apotheosis 76, 77, 139
Aquaman 14, 172, 173
Aragorn viii
Arawn 154, 155
Arthur, King viii, 6, 9, 14, 24, 34, 112, 165–8, 171
Augustus 77
Autumn Equinox 94, 176, 182, 183

Ballyvadlea 129
Barnabas 138, 139
Bath 134
Beauty and the Beast 4, 5, 8, 11–13, 52, 125, 164
Bedouin 44, 45
Beltane 69, 91, 178–80
Bible, the 135, 136, 138, 139
Billy Goats Gruff 38, 39, 49
Blacksmiths 12, 13, 88, 171, 183
Blithe Spirit 144
'Bog bodies' 15, 90–2, 146–8, 151, 153, 151–62

Boudicca 76, 89, 95–8, 135, 136, 177, 178
Bran the Blessed 110, 111
Bride 177, 178
Brigid 177, 178
Broddenbjerg idol 68–70
Bronze Age xi, 8, 9, 12, 14, 17, 19, 26, 30, 33, 37–9, 43, 69, 78, 93, 121, 164, 165, 171, 172, 175

Caesar, Julius 77, 133
Calendar 27, 28, 52, 94, 95 175–86
Camelot 167, 168
Candlemas 178
Cap o' Rushes 16, 17
Catholic Church 80, 87, 110
Cauldrons 60, 61, 102, 105–12, 165
Causewayed enclosures 47, 48, 58
Celtic Fringe ix, 128
Celts 61, 65, 84, 89, 91, 97, 100, 101, 106, 107, 131, 134
Cernunnos 60, 61, 84, 85, 109, 140, 142
Christianity 12, 71, 86, 111, 132–46, 177, 180, 181
Christmas 27, 175, 176, 185
Chronicles of Narnia 169

Cinderella 22, 23
Cleary, Bridget and Michael 129–31
Cornwall 128, 129
Coward, Noel 144
Crowley, Alistair 147

Dagenham Idol 67–71
Deae Matronae 50
Deer 57, 58, 61, 62, 68, 82, 83, 109, 127
Devil, Christian 56, 57, 66, 86, 132, 138, 140, 141
Diana 83
Disney films 164
Drowning, 15, 89, 151, 153, 156–62
Druids 91–3, 95, 134
Duncan, Helen 144–6, 162, 185

Easter 27, 178
Eddas 37, 71–4, 76
Excalibur 6, 9, 24, 31, 32, 171

Fabian, Robert 155, 156, 160, 161
Fairies 8, 10, 17, 19, 52, 114–31, 167
Fairy forts 128–30
Fairy tales xi, 2, 5, 9–24, 41, 48, 49, 123, 125, 164, 165, 168
Father Christmas 38, 73–5, 162, 174
Faust 12
Feast of the Purification 178
Flood, great 121–3
Flores 123–5

Fogous 128, 129
Folk memories 24–39, 63, 73, 112, 121
Fonts 110, 111
Fountains 32, 39, 72, 174
Fraudulent Mediums Act 1951 145
Frazer, James 56
Frodo Baggins viii

Game of Thrones viii, xi, 2, 4, 48, 171, 173
Gandalf viii–x, 4, 34, 37, 73, 76, 104, 112
Gardner, Gerald 147
Geoffrey of Monmouth 34–6
Goats 38, 44, 45, 49, 57, 66, 74, 75, 185
Grimes Graves 58
Grimm, Brothers 41, 42, 84, 165
Grimm's Fairy Tales 2, 15, 16
Groundhog Day 28, 177
Gundestrup Cauldron 60, 61, 85, 108–11, 132

Halloween 182–4
Hansel and Gretel 20, 23
Hares 96, 97, 178
Haroldskaer Woman 157, 158
Harry Potter viii, 14, 112, 166, 172–4
Harvest Festival 182
Heart, stake through 158, 159, 162

Hedingham witchcraft case 151, 152
Herne the Hunter 83–5, 165, 168
Hochdorf 107
Holy Grail 111, 112, 168
Homeopathy 56
Homer 17, 25, 53, 70
Horned animals 57–65
Horned God 54–67, 81, 141, 185
Horned man 60–4
Horne, Janet 143
Houses of Parliament 164–6
Human sacrifice 147–63
Hunting 2, 54, 55, 59, 60, 62–4, 80–6, 97

Ice Age in Europe 44, 48, 54, 122
Idylls of the King 167
Iliad 17, 25, 26, 53, 66
Imbolc 28, 175–8
Indo-European language 12, 21, 40–3, 71, 108, 132
Indo-European people 20, 39–54, 66, 99, 100, 107, 125, 128, 132
Irminsul 68
Iron Age 15, 30, 31, 90, 97, 159–61

Jack and the Beanstalk 12, 21, 22, 48
Jack o' Lantern 183
Jane Eyre 10, 11, 13, 114, 115
Jones, William 40
Joseph of Arimathea 112

Julian calendar 175
Jupiter 133

Krampus 74, 75, 185

Lady of Shallot 167
Lady of the Lake 7, 9, 31, 32
Lapps 59
La Tène 30
Lewis, C.S. 4, 87, 114, 169, 170
Lindow Man 90, 92
Little People 5, 8, 10, 19, 53, 113–31, 172
Little Red Riding Hood 10
Lithuania 20, 21, 41, 71
London 7, 29–33, 67, 68, 142, 158, 159, 166, 167
Lord of the Animals 64, 65, 74, 80, 84, 85, 109, 132
Lugnasad 27, 182
Lupercalia 178
Lystra 139

Macbeth 49, 106
Maleficent 2, 29
Mallory, Thomas 4, 34, 112, 165
Mammoth 58, 59
Mars 133
Mass 133
Maxwell, Jean 143
May Day 178–80
Maypoles 69, 180
Mead 108

Mediums 135, 143–6
Meon Hill 154, 155
Mercury 133
Merlin viii, 14, 24, 34, 35, 37, 162, 165, 166, 169, 170
Middle Earth 5, 165
Midsummer's Day 176, 181, 182
Midsummer Night's Dream 105, 114, 181
Mimir 72
Mistletoe 92
Mithras 142
Morris, William 167
Murray, Margaret 84, 147

Narnia 29
Neanderthals 47, 57, 58, 81
Necromancy 142
Neolithic Age 37, 47, 69, 78, 118–21, 164, 176
Newgrange tomb 28
New Year's Day 175
Noah's Ark 121
Numinor 169

Odin 37, 38, 53, 70–3, 75–7, 84, 85, 88–91, 141, 184–6
One-eyed god 69, 70, 75, 141
Osborn, Ruth 150, 151

Palaeolithic Age 14, 63, 103, 105
Pan 60, 64
Paphos 138

Parsees 47
Parsifal 168
Paul, apostle 138–40
Peter Pan 114
Pillar of the Boatmen 61
Pole gods 68, 69, 180
Pratchett, Terry 4
Pre-Raphaelite Brotherhood 167

Q-Anon shaman 62
Quinn, Sean 131

Rapunzel 20, 21, 116, 137
Ratcliffe Highway Murders 159
Rebecca 13
Red Lady of Paviland 105
Reindeer 38, 59, 64, 74, 75
Religion 6, 29, 51, 53, 60, 87, 88, 103, 132–4, 142
Reykjavik ix
Ring of the Nibelung 168
Rip Van Winkle xi
Romano-Celtic temples 133, 134
Romulus and Remus 14
Rule of Three 19, 48–51, 89, 134
Rumpelstiltskin 8, 11, 17–19, 116, 125

Sacrifices, weapons and money 6, 7, 9, 29, 30, 32, 33
St John's Wort 181, 182
Samhain 27, 175, 182, 183
Sanskrit 40, 41, 51

Santa Claus 185
Saturnalia 184
School holidays 27–9, 174, 175, 185
Shamans 62, 63, 65–7, 80–2
Silbury Hill 46
Sleipnir 37
Sleeping Beauty 164
Snow White 4, 22, 23, 164
Sorcerer of Trois-Frères 59–61, 63, 74, 82, 84, 85
Southwark Cathedral 33, 142
Spring Equinox 27, 28, 94, 176, 178, 185
Star Carr 61
Step-parents 22, 23
Stonehenge 35, 36, 45, 46, 180
Strabo 134, 135
Swords, naming of 170–2
Sympathetic magic 56, 63, 80, 179

Taklimata Desert 100
Taranis 89, 109, 133
Tarot 143
Tennant, Ann 152–4
Tennyson, Alfred Lord 32, 112, 167
Thames, River 7, 29, 30, 65
That Hideous Strength 169, 170
The Borrowers 117, 118
The Gallic Wars 133
The Golden Bough 56
The Hobbit viii, 169, 170
The Lion, the Witch and the Wardrobe xi, 2, 104, 169

The Lord of the Rings viii, x, xi, 2, 5, 10, 34, 73, 112, 117, 168–70
The Merry Wives of Windsor 83
The Singing Bone 15
The Smith and the Devil 12, 13
The Song of Roland 171
The Sound of Music 13, 14
The Sword in the Stone 169, 173
The Three Little Pigs 16
The Wizard of Oz x
Theseus 14
Thor 74, 75, 88
Threefold death 89, 90
Tolkien, J.R.R. viii, x, 10, 73, 87
Torcs 61
Tring 103, 149, 150
Trojan War 25, 26, 66, 67

Ukraine 12, 43, 122, 127

Vauxhall 29, 30
Veleda 136, 137
Vestal Virgins 137
Victoria, Queen 166, 167
Victorian Era 166, 167
Voodoo 56

Wagner, Richard 87, 168, 169
Walpurgis Night 178–80
Walton, Charles 154–7, 159–61
Wands and staffs 3, 6, 33, 37, 73, 78, 102–05, 112, 152
Waun Mawn 36

Wenham, Jane 148-9
Wheeler, Mortimer 110
Wild Hunt 54, 80–6, 154, 165, 168
Winter Solstice 27–9, 37, 57, 73, 84, 93, 176, 182, 184, 185
Witchcraft Act 1735 143–5
Witchcraft, prohibition of 135–46
Witches:
   appearance of ix, x, 95, 98–101, 113, 174
   behaviour of viii, 3, 20, 97, 98, 105, 106, 132, 136, 137, 157, 158
Witches of Subeshi 100
Wizards:
   appearance of viii–x, 3, 6, 7, 27, 37, 52, 73, 78
   archetype 34, 37, 66, 68–79, 85
   behaviour of 3, 18, 30, 31, 34, 39, 51, 52, 65, 87–101, 136, 172
   hats of viii–x, 6, 27, 52, 76, 93–5
Woden, Wotan, *see* Odin

Yamnaya 39–54, 107, 109, 119, 120, 125, 126, 132, 179
Yggdrasil Tree 72, 89, 90
Yule 37, 38, 73
Yule Father 37, 38, 73–5, 185

Zeus 67, 133, 139